Endorsements

One of the most unusual things I've ever seen in my life has been to watch God release an anointing for writing on so many of our staff members at Bethel Church. Each one has something unique and powerful to add to the overall picture of what God is saying in this hour. *An Apple a Day* will be a great encouragement to you as you glean from the wisdom of a host of authors who love the move of God and enjoy the privilege of being a part of a community of believers.

> Bill Johnson, Senior Pastor
> Bethel Church, Redding, CA
> Author of *When Heaven Invades Earth* and
> *Hosting the Presence*

As a surgeon I read many books, most have to do with the physical and emotional aspects of health. My wife and I lead a ministry that raises Kingdom leaders in the marketplace. As far as that part of my calling, I read many books on spiritual matters. I have not encountered a book that so beautifully deals with all aspects of humanity, the body soul and spirit. Pam Spinosi has assembled a heartfelt group of authors that touch on all aspects of life. Physical, emotion, relational, family, intellectual and spiritual health are all skillfully explored in this book. This current revival movement needs Christians who are whole in body, soul and spirit. Pam's book takes readers one- step closer to that goal.

> Theodore Sawchuk, MD, FACS
> Physician, surgeon, and revivalist
> Fargo, ND

Destiny Image Books by Pam Spinosi

An Apple for the Road

AN APPLE A DAY

Health in Every Realm

Compiled by
PAM SPINOSI

DESTINY IMAGE® PUBLISHERS, INC.
P.O. Box 310, Shippensburg, PA 17257-0310

"Promoting Inspired Lives."

This book and all other Destiny Image, Revival Press, MercyPlace, Fresh Bread, Destiny Image Fiction, and Treasure House books are available at Christian bookstores and distributors worldwide.

For a U.S. bookstore nearest you, call 1-800-722-6774.

For more information on foreign distributors, call 717-532-3040.

Reach us on the Internet: www.destinyimage.com.

ISBN 13 TP: 978-0-7684-4222-9

ISBN 13 Ebook: 978-0-7684-8574-5

For Worldwide Distribution, Printed in the U.S.A.

1 2 3 4 5 6 7 8 / 17 16 15 14 13

Contents

FAMILY HEALTH
CHAPTER 5

RELATIONAL HEALTH
CHAPTER 6

CREATIVE HEALTH
CHAPTER 7

FINANCIAL HEALTH
CHAPTER 8

INTELLECTUAL HEALTH
CHAPTER 9

THE HEALTH OF CHILDLIKENESS
CHAPTER 10

Foreword

I don't particularly like the use of the word *balance* to describe perspectives or beliefs as the "balance" often involves compromise or a dilution of passion. It is, however, balance which comes to mind as I read this wonderful book. Not the balance of compromise but the articulation of many ways to become healthy or help someone else on their journey to a healthier lifestyle. Every chapter stands alone, but every perspective also needs the other perspectives to achieve the life that Jesus wants for us all.

As I read, what excited me most was that I realized that I know all the authors and for the most part, *really* know them. Because I know them, I can tell you that their chapters are real expressions of not merely what they think or teach, but how they live. They are nearly all life messages to some extent or another, and each one of them makes a contribution to the culture of Bethel. Each one, by the way they live, work and minister in the incredibly busy and exciting environment of Bethel Church is living what you will read. As I run down the list of chapters in my mind, I can see and hear each person, and I begin to see afresh their unique contribution to the move of God of which Bethel is a part. Without each expression, there would be something missing, and if only one was emphasized, we would be in danger of becoming a cult. It is the interplay of individuals who carry a passion for an aspect of healthy Kingdom living which is creating a "whole" movement in the same way as it will create a "whole" you as you read and digest it. This book is a unique perspective and comes in the context of the most important subject of our lives: Health. But, as you will read, it comes not with a narrow perspective but a broad one, not tasteless but full of rich flavor. This is not a blend, but a diverse menu waiting to be enjoyed.

I am certain that there are lessons for all of us from every chapter, but I want to also encourage you to find the voice or voices with which you resonate and give yourself permission to specialize a little! Perhaps there is an emphasis which you need for a season, or maybe as you read the Lord will give you permission to teach or minister or live with a greater emphasis on one "health" focus. Each author has many expressions, but at the same time, their chapters are not as much of a surprise when you know them. Being known for something is in itself healthy and opens new doors of relationships and opportunities.

Perhaps this book demands a new definition of *balanced*: The ability to carry more weight without toppling over. I believe that this will be the result for the reader, an ability to grow in an area of your healthy life and as you do, rather than become unbalanced, you will become more able to carry this newfound weight or emphasis, and thus, the other areas of your life will become healthier, too!

Paul Manwaring

Introduction

"*Sahtein,*" my Syrian grandmother would say after I had downed another helping of her scrumptious home-cooked goodness. *Sahtein,* a blessing pronounced after a meal, means "two healths," the reply to which is translated, "on your heart." I'm not sure exactly what the expression "two healths" refers to, but I always found the idea of "two healths" intriguing. I like to think it means physical *and* spiritual health. It could also mean "double health." I'll take all the health I can get!

The idea behind this book is that our God, who promised us life more abundantly, loves to give us health in *all* the areas of our lives. So I asked others to write about a particular area of health they are enjoying in hopes of encouraging others to pursue health in many realms.

I hope you will be blessed as you read it, and from my heart, I wish you *Sahtein*!

Pam Spinosi

INNER HEALTH

—CHAPTER 1—

It is for freedom that Christ has set us free. Stand firm, then, and do not let yourselves be burdened again by a yoke of slavery (Gal. 5:1 NIV).

Freedom! What a wonderful word. I think freedom may be one of the values dearest to the American soul. As an American, I have always enjoyed political, religious, and personal freedom, but I am aware that the greatest freedom lies not outside of us, but inside. The freedom from sin and all the emotions that go with it—fear, guilt, rejection, to name a few—is greater than all the other precious kinds of liberty. Only one source of that freedom exists: the Lord Jesus. But how to enter into the liberty of the Lord eludes many. So I have asked to write this first chapter one who has seen hundreds set free. Connection with each person of the Trinity is the basis for spiritual health. And that spiritual health opens the door to health in other areas of our lives. Let's start at the beginning and explore together health in many realms. —P.S.

Body, Soul, and Spirit Healing

by Dawna De Silva

We spend so much time and money bolstering our self-image with gyms, salads, creams, and even plastic surgery that we forget that lasting beauty isn't found in pills and creams, and that true love doesn't cost us membership dues. We punish our bodies, deny them comfort, and then expect our bodies to thank us in the morning. It's no wonder our bodies hold us hostage to physical pain, sickness, and torment. But Jesus, the lover of our souls, sets us free, and releases our body, soul, and spirit to soar. Our lives are *"renewed like the eagle's"* (Ps. 103:5 NIV). We rejoice like *"calves [released] from the stall"* (Mal. 4:2 AMP), and our bodies get the benefit of walking no longer *"according to the flesh, but according to the spirit"* (Rom. 8:1).

So how do we heal our souls so that our spirits and bodies walk in freedom? We reach into the caverns of our pain-filled emptiness and open our hearts to the One who redeems. I have seen it consistently over my years in the Sozo Ministry. People come discouraged, degraded, caught in their cycles of addiction and fear. But when they spend time meeting with Jesus, the Father, and the Holy Spirit, they leave restored. Jesus tells us, *"Come to me, all you who...are heavy laden, and I will give you rest...rest for your souls"* (Matt. 11:28-29).

We can only experience true freedom once we have lowered our defenses and encountered Christ. A simple prayer and walkthrough of forgiveness can bring healing to our bodies, souls, and spirits. Here is an example:

I ask my body to forgive me for any negative self-talk I have done and for any harmful words that I or others have spoken over my health. I ask my body to forgive me for the times I "tuned out" in order to endure the years of abuse, where my body stayed present while my mind and emotions were allowed to be safely tucked away. And I release my body from having to hold the trauma and the memories of fear and harm. I repent for all negative words I have spoken over myself, and I release to you, Jesus, all self-hatred, belittlement, sexual immorality, and shame. I invite you, body, to release the anger, bitterness, hopelessness, and pain to Jesus, and I thank you, Jesus, for the sacrifice of your blood. I invite you, Holy Spirit, to reach into my spirit and break off of my body all residues of fear, hopelessness, self-sufficiency, and trauma.

Once such prayers are released, physical healing begins to flow. Tears of pain transform to joy, muscles relax, pain ceases, hopelessness collapses, and love again reigns strong!

LIES

So what weighs us down? What makes us feel heavy-laden? Some of you might think, "Chocolate? Carbs?" Although these might be what add weight to the morning scale, the lies we have learned to believe about ourselves are what truly plague our bodies, souls, and spirits. Buried deep inside are lies that we have joined with and even repeated throughout our daily lives to such an extent that they have taken root as "truths." These lies fester in our souls, bringing worry, fear, hatred, anger, physical sickness, and pain, bending us toward hollow ways of trying to combat these beliefs inside of us. Not until we meet Jesus face to face are we able to gain complete victory over these voices.

Does this sound familiar? Here are some lies you may or may not believe:

One: "But you don't understand. I have been battling anger all my life. I learned it as a child from my dad. I know it is destructive, but it's all I have ever known. I have prayed about it for years, and I get better, but in time something will come up and I will just blow."

Two: "I have been in ministry for over 30 years, but I continue to be stuck in a cycle of pornography. I know that God forgives me, and I do really well for a while. Invariably, however, the temptation comes and even though I struggle to fight it off, it finally gets so strong that I give up fighting it. Over and over I repent from the shame of my moral failure, and although Jesus forgives and restores me, I am ashamed and exhausted from this moral failure that I hide from my congregation and my family."

Three: "I have been a believer for many years, but I just can't stop the voices that ridicule me. I don't feel the joy that everyone tells me I should feel, and I can't find peace."

Four: "I'm in pain every day of my life, and I just can't take it anymore."

These lies of the enemy penetrate deep into our core and begin ravaging our bodies, strangling our souls, and squashing our spirits. They take hold of our emotions and our reason and develop into thought structures whose roots invade the fabric of our minds until we no longer see truth clearly. We begin to filter every encounter through these mindsets. It is why God tells us to take *"every thought captive to the obedience of Christ"* (2 Cor. 10:5 NASB). It is why knowing the Word of God is so valuable—for the Word combats the enemy's lies by showing us the truth. And it is here, in the lie structures, that we must allow the truth to enter, to take up residence in previously hostile territory, and to unravel old patterns and weave in strong, everlasting ties to our God, our Father, and our King.

Here are some important truths to remember: we are not helpless, we are not victims, and we were not given a spirit of fear (see 2 Tim. 1:7). We were created in the image of a loving, awesome, and powerful God. He did not forsake us. He did not abandon us to simply survive. Instead, He sent His Son to provide a way of escape for us—to redeem us and to restore us to our rightful place (see Rom. 8:15). In Him, we are powerful victors winning daily battles, courageous warriors tearing down strongholds (see 2 Cor. 10:4), and fully equipped believers walking in both power and love. Every time you feel a lie counteract any of these biblical truths, you must stop and renounce it right away. Do not let these lies fester any longer in your soul.

Breaking off Lies

Lie-busting prayers do not need to be anything spectacular. Often we simply need to release forgiveness to family members who have caused harm to us in the past, whether they meant to cause us pain or not. Sometimes all we have to do as believers is take our unforgiveness, hurt, and offense before God and let Him take care of the rest. Simply put, we get to let go of pain and let God be King.

Here are examples of simple prayers that can break off lies:

One: *"I ask you, God, to forgive me for the judgments I have made against my father, and I choose to forgive my dad for every missed 'Atta boy,' every broken promise, and every memory of disinterest. I forgive him for being so wrapped up in himself that he didn't have anything left to give his family, and I release him from not being a father whom I could draw strength from. I renounce the lie that you, Father God, are disinterested in my life and that you are busy taking on the world's problems and don't have any time left for me. I hand to you, Father God, rejection, isolation, loneliness, performance, and self-sufficiency. What do you give me in exchange?"*

Two: *"I choose to forgive my mom for making me feel like I could never do anything right, and I renounce the lie that you, Holy Spirit, are just waiting to correct me. I hand to you, Holy Spirit, a critical spirit, self-belittlement, performance, and perfectionism. What do you want to give me in exchange for these things?"*

Three: *"I ask you to forgive me, Lord, for opening a door to sexual sin. I renounce all participation with pornography, fantasy, and perversion. I invite you, Jesus, to wash me clean, and I hand to you self-hatred, anger, perversion, and shame, and I close the door to sexual sin in Jesus' name. What do you have for me in exchange?"*

Once the lie is identified and the person is forgiven, it is now time to renounce the lie that God is in some way at fault or capable of inflicting this same pain. Then it's a matter of seeing what God has for them in return. What's truly amazing about God is He always knows what to give the person, and He knows what best method should be used in order to communicate that truth.

Heirs

A powerful truth to recognize when wanting to heal our body, soul, and spirit is that we are not slaves (see Rom. 8:15). We are powerful heirs with Christ. He redeemed us from Adam's sin so that we are no longer outcasts but joint heirs. (See Eph. 2:19.) The cross reconciled us to our Father. Once we realize this, all the enemy's lies begin to lose their power because we realize that we have the authority to overcome them. That's when we begin to walk in freedom. It is within the Father's embrace that we find our identity, our structure, our courage, and that is what the enemy has been trying to keep us from.

ORPHAN SPIRIT

We are also not orphans. The orphan spirit tells us that we are alone, that no one will come through for us and that we have to take care of it all ourselves. Performance, perfectionism and self-sufficiency begin to own us as fear becomes our master. To counter fear, which we know as good Christians God did not give us (see 2 Tim. 1:7), many times we align ourselves with a spirit of control. This control gives us a false sense of security until reality strikes and we realize just how little we do control, and so begins the swing between the extremes of fear and control. We don't want to be afraid, so we take control. Control lets us down, so we become afraid. These cycles scream at us that "God is not protecting us. He is disinterested in our daily lives." Or quite simply, "God doesn't work!"

SONS

> *If you then, being evil, know how to give good gifts to your children, how much more will your Father who is in heaven give good things to those who ask Him* (Matt. 7:11).

One of the most damaging lies to our souls is that God is not good and that He is waiting for us to mess up so He can punish us. What this lie implies is that we have to constantly be on guard against His response to our actions, which keeps us focused not on Him, but on ourselves. We find such freedom when we are not looking at every action for punishment but are looking to His face for His reaction to us. From this position, we respond to His love with proper lifestyles of worship and holiness, for it is in beholding His face that we are spurred on "to be holy, even as He is holy." (See 1 Peter 1:16.) It is in these moments with the Father that we begin to mimic what we see until the world actually can recognize His attributes in us. We begin to take on the characteristics of our Father in Heaven, and we are able to see ourselves no longer as orphaned travelers of this world but ambassadors of Christ.

GOD'S VOICE

Sometimes a Sozo client will say, "I can't hear God's voice. I have been a Christian a really long time, and I am so frustrated." Within a few minutes of interacting with them, I come to the conclusion that because of their disappointments or hardships in life, trauma they have experienced, or prior failed relationships, they have constructed opinions about God and have erected walls that prevent them from hearing His voice. I recognize that the lie most likely was formed in their early childhood and after answering a few questions, I have the client repeat:

> *I forgive my dad for yelling at me and making me feel like I could never get anything right, and I renounce the lie that you, Father God, are just going to yell at me if I were to hear your voice. I hand to you, Father God, a spirit of fear, performance, and self-hatred, and I give you permission to take my hands away from my ears and to speak to me. Father God, what truth do you want me to know?*

The answer can be something like this: "Love. Acceptance. Peace. Rest." A huge weight lifts off the client's shoulders. They usually say that they feel lighter and their bodies actually release the pent up tension they had been carrying.

Then I tend to follow up with this question: "Father God, what do you think of me?"

The client usually can't believe what they hear at first. But it is truth and it can take time to sink in: *"You are my beloved. You are my treasure. You are my friend."*

Once we allow God to speak, we are able to filter out lies and plant truths in their place. We must not just add good seed to bad soil. We need to supplant the old crop with new. Planting truths over lies will mask what we believe and make us look healthier for a while, but it won't stop the inner torment or embarrassing eruptions of ungodly behavior, *"...for out of the abundance of the heart the mouth speaks"* (Matt. 12:34). Roots must be pulled if we are going to get rid of the weeds, and new seeds must be sown if we want a new garden to emerge. You cannot get good fruit out of a bad tree. (See Luke 6:43.)

But God is still the healer, the redeemer, the comforter, and our strength. He is wisdom and truth and He *can* and *will* heal us and set us free!

It will take courage to open up to Jesus the things you hold secretly deep down inside. It will take belief that God will not reject you when He sees you as you truly are. And it will take the strength God has given you to pull yourself up out of the pit you are in and embrace freedom. If you ever feel powerless and unable to rise up, declare courage to your spirit. Tell it to rise up and grab your soul by the lapels and shake it, and declare that God is good and is not a rejecter of those who diligently seek Him. Speak strength to your physical body to be able to combat any disease, all fatigue, all heaviness, any chemical imbalances, and all mental torment. And declare it in Jesus' name.

COMBATING LIES

There are many ways to uproot the lies. Reading the Word can cause an epiphany that brings us out of the doldrums of believing false truth. In reading God's truths we are reminded of what we should believe and follow. (See Prov. 7:1-3.) Sometimes just putting these words before our eyes shocks our brains into a "reset," an "Oh yeah, that's who He is and that's who He says I am," and challenges us to open up to prior foreign possibilities.

Another way to review truth is in sharing testimonies of what God has done. The Israelites demonstrated this by setting up memorial stones along the way so that they would be able to point out to their children where exactly God showed up for the past generations. (See Ex. 28:12.) This was used to show the children God's faithfulness to prior generations and as an encouragement that the God who was with their fathers would also be with them.

Words of encouragement and prophetic declarations over us from other believers also help combat the lies we believe about ourselves. When people speak into our lives as

God sees us, it makes us question the way we see ourselves. These words help to open up possibilities in our minds that maybe we have a purpose after all and lend credence to our inner dreams. We begin to hope, and in hoping we desire to become who God already says we are.

Sometimes, however, the lies we are believing are so embedded in us that we read only condemnation in the Word of God, we scoff at how God has supposedly come through for others while clearly forgetting us, and when encouraging, prophetic words are spoken over us, we roll our eyes and think, "Yeah, if they only knew who they were really prophesying over." In times like this, we must open up our inner belief systems to the truth and allow Him to speak truth over us. What may seem ridiculous may actually be truth. In such seasons of frustration and mental combat fatigue, it can be extremely useful to seek out help in rooting out these lie structures.

There is no shame in asking for help in these seasons. I find that outsiders see the lies we are believing a lot more easily than we are able to see them ourselves. They are able to stand outside our circumstances and view our lives from a non-emotional state and are able to speak to our core systems truths that we, ourselves, would not be able to take in on our own. In these times of ministry, we come face to face with the tangled web of deceit that the enemy has woven into the fabric of our lives and thus into our relationships. This is where we pull on the courage God placed in our spirits and open up the hidden chambers of our hearts to the light of His Son. This is where we choose to forgive the offenders in our lives and break all inner vows we have made because of these offenses. This is where we allow the Holy Spirit to remove our pain and begin to nurture us with His truth. And this is where we begin to walk out freedom!

INTERCONNECTED

Because our body, soul, and spirit are intertwined, it should not come as a shock that each of these unique parts of us can cause disruptions to the others. Our bodies are in pain so we begin feeling angry, sad, or depressed. We feel grumpy so we run that extra mile, work out harder, and take it out on our body. We feel less spiritual than the others around us so we bounce from conference to conference, staying up late into the wee hours, denying our bodies the rest they need. I have found that this disunity between the body, soul, and spirit can cause physical sickness, emotional distress, and a disempowering of our spirits.

It is important, therefore, to make sure that each part of us—body, soul, and spirit—are healthy and at peace. When our bodies are out of whack, we need to rest, and when we come down with sickness, we should get prayer for physical healing. When our spirits are dejected, we need to worship, spend time in His Word, and soak in prayer so that we can fill our spirits back up full. When our souls are following lies, we must take these lies captive and ask God to impart into us His truth. Each of these can happen alone with God or with outside help. Outwardly, we worship at church and it lifts up our spirits, we go to doctors for medicine to help our bodies fight disease or go to healing rooms and watch God heal our broken bones, and we can go to counselors and inner healing/deliverance ministers to heal our burdened souls.

Healing of our body, soul and spirit is our birthright in Christ.

EMOTIONAL HEALTH

—CHAPTER 2—

...whom having not seen you love. Though now you do not see Him, yet believing, you rejoice with joy inexpressible and full of glory (1 Pet. 1:8).

I once heard a comedian talking about his work with a deep sense of purpose. He knew he was helping people—and he was. I read somewhere about a man who watched funny movies as his therapy for his illness, and it was working. I have a relative who combats stress in the same way. No one would dispute the therapeutic value of laughter and joy. Volumes have been written about it in medical circles. We know we can boost our immune system by staying joyful. Maybe it's one reason the Lord asks us to rejoice; He knows it's good for us. Joy is also the environment He lives in and the feeling He spreads, and His joy is higher than anything we can get from a movie. It fulfills and transforms; it comes with His presence. Without question, unfeigned, uncontainable joy is a sure sign of spiritual health. The next author lives his conviction about the essentialness of joy. And he takes it beyond personal benefit to seeing joy and laughter as a means of releasing the healing power of God to others. He has unusual testimonies, such as laughing over a critically ill person, causing her to laugh, rip out her oxygen tubes and dash around the church—healed!

Sometimes joy begins as a choice. So put a smile on your face as you get ready to read this next chapter. —P.S.

Good Medicine: Taking Your Daily Dose of Vitamin J

by Kevin Dedmon

Recently, a former graduate of Firestarters (a 12-week class I developed to fast-track people into a supernatural life-style) returned to the class crying because she had been diagnosed with lymphoma, a type of cancer. She had a huge tumor protruding from the side of her neck and was in tremendous pain as she came into the class that Sunday morning.

The doctors had pronounced her condition hopeless, instructing her to go home and prepare for death. Being a single mother of three children (all under the age of seven), and having no other family members competent to take the children, she was devastated with the prognosis.

Upon hearing the news and seeing the lemon-sized tumor, one of our Firestarters overseers suggested that we have the entire class pray over her for a miracle. Immediately, the class was instructed to extend their hands toward the woman and laugh. The class of about 80 students proceeded to laugh for about five minutes in celebration of God's goodness toward the woman.

During the laugh session, the same overseer was impressed to have the woman drink a glass of water. Halfway through the glass of water, the woman began to gag and then began to cough up chunks of the tumor into the trashcan. The entire class looked on in amazement (and revulsion) as the tumor shrank until it was no longer noticeable. The woman began crying, then shouting praises to God, and then laughing hysterically as she declared that all of the pain was gone!

A few weeks later, she had additional testing. The doctors were completely confounded because all of the tests confirmed that she no longer had any signs of a tumor or cancer!

In Proverbs 17:22, Solomon provides a promising prescription for a healthy life. He says that, *"A cheerful heart is good medicine...."* The word "cheerful," as translated in the New International Version, is the Hebrew word *sameach*, which means "glad," "joyful," "merry," or "rejoicing." I propose that laughing is an integral element and manifestation of joy, and that laughter is essential to cultivating a "merry" heart, resulting in spiritual, emotional, and physical wellbeing.

As a physician's assistant (I assist the Great Physician by taking risks), I have prescribed laughter to thousands of people who have been miraculously healed in response to the presence and power of God that is released in Kingdom joy. I believe that laughter acts as a lubricant, enabling the works of God to be activated in a person's life or circumstances.

Isaiah promised that Jesus, the Messiah, would bring the *"oil of gladness,"* and *"everlasting joy"* (Isa. 61:3,7 NASB). In Luke 6:21, Jesus promised that those who received the Kingdom of God would continually laugh.

Even Jesus was anointed with the oil of joy (see Heb. 1:9 NIV). In other words, it was the joy that enabled and empowered Him to accomplish the mission of releasing the Kingdom of God from Heaven to earth. If Jesus needed the oil of joy to confirm the message with signs and wonders and miracles (see Heb. 2:3-4), then it stands to reason that we also need a daily dose of joy in order to walk in supernatural Kingdom life, experiencing physical, emotional, relational, and spiritual wholeness.

Every believer would do well to remember to take a dose of "Vitamin J" each day. The joy of the Lord is our strength/empowerment (see Neh. 8:10), which is why I believe the apostle Paul instructed us to always be joyful (see 1 Thess. 5:16 NLT).

Joy is good medicine.

Many studies have been done to demonstrate how joy and laughter improve both emotional and physical health. The following article highlights some of the research that has promoted the benefits of joy and laughter related to our wellbeing:

> Dr. Lee Berk, an immunologist at Loma Linda University's School of Allied Health and Medicine, has studied the effects of mirthful laughter on the regulation of hormones since the 1980s. Berk and his colleagues found that laughter helps the brain regulate the stress hormones cortisol and epinephrine. They also discovered a link between laughter and the production of anti-bodies and endorphins, the body's natural painkillers. Even the expectation

that something funny is coming suffices to bring about positive effects, reports Dr. Berk.

Humor also helps the brain regulate the brain's dopamine levels, reports a Stanford research team in the December 4, 2003, issue of the journal Neuron. Dopamine, also known as "the reward hormone," is a neurotransmitter that regulates mood, motivation, attention and learning.[1]

God knew long before medical science that laughter is a major key to wholeness and wellbeing. He knew that the best medicine for humankind was a merry heart—joy. People who live in laughter have a higher hope for a healthier life. In addition, I have found that I have experienced a much higher success rate in supernatural physical healing as I have cultivated a lifestyle of laughter.

CREATING A HEALTHY ATMOSPHERE FOR CREATIVE MIRACLES

After the first evening meeting of a Supernatural Lifestyle conference that I was conducting in Speyer, Germany, a husband approached me asking if I would be willing to pray for his wife, who had a completely paralyzed leg. She had been through several surgeries and many hours of physical therapy with no success. The medical team had finally declared her disabled for life and designed a $10,000 custom brace to stabilize her leg from the hip to her foot so that she could at least hobble around with the aid of crutches or a walker.

I had just been teaching that night about how risk releases us into our supernatural destiny, and that we have to be willing to go beyond our comfort level in order for an action to be considered risk. In other words, if there is no possibility of failure or danger, we cannot say that we are taking risk. I taught that we must have a "chicken line" if we are going to go to new levels of releasing the supernatural power of God in people's lives. So, I told the man that I would be happy to attempt the impossible!

About twenty people gathered around as the word spread that I was going to try and release a miracle on the woman's leg. I could sense the expectancy of the small crowd as I explained that we were going to see a miracle, but as I began to minister to the woman, the onlookers began crying out to God with wailing, pleading prayers, accented with severely strained, sad countenances. I could feel the faith evaporate from the room.

I instantly thought of a similar situation that Jesus found himself in Mark 5:35-43:

> *While Jesus was still speaking, some men came from the house of Jairus, the synagogue ruler. "Your daughter is dead," they said. "Why bother the teacher any more?" Ignoring what they said, Jesus told the synagogue ruler, "Don't be afraid; just believe." He did not let anyone follow him except Peter, James and John the brother of James. When they came to the home of the synagogue ruler, Jesus saw a commotion, with people crying and wailing loudly. He went in and said to them, "Why all this commotion and wailing? The child is not dead but asleep." But they laughed at him. After he put them all out, he took the child's father and mother and the disciples who were with*

him, and went in where the child was. He took her by the hand and said to her, "Talitha koum!" (which means, "Little girl, I say to you, get up!"). Immediately the girl stood up and walked around (she was twelve years old). At this they were completely astonished. He gave strict orders not to let anyone know about this, and told them to give her something to eat (Mark 5:35-43 NIV).

Notice that Jesus asked all of the mourners to leave. I believe it was because crying and wailing is antithetical to faith—weeping and wailing is not good medicine.

Jesus needed an environment of faith in order to release the supernatural power of God to bring about resurrection life in this twelve-year-old girl. Similarly, I needed to change the atmosphere, so I politely instructed the onlookers that they were welcome to observe as long as they agreed to smile as a minimum and laugh if possible.

A few left with scowls on their faces.

Like Jesus, I have learned that it is better to have a few believers gathered who are full of faith rather than many mourners who have succumbed to the finality of fatalistic thinking. While mourning is an appropriate response to the effects of sin and death, it is not appropriate in the environment of faith. Obviously, Jesus did not condemn the mourners who were crying and wailing, but He did not want their response to death to impact the environment of faith He was attempting to create.

So He asked the mourners to leave.

If we want more of the power of God in and through our lives, then we must have more of the presence of God in and through our lives. It is the presence of God that contains and releases the power of God. In God's presence, anything is possible.

The Scripture is clear: *"In Your presence is fullness of joy..."* (Ps. 16:11 NASB). While weeping and wailing is a reality of the environment of this world, it is not characteristic of the reality of Heaven and the Kingdom of God. The medicine of Heaven is joy, gladness, and merriment.

I returned my focus to the woman's paralyzed leg and began to laugh over it. I noticed an elderly woman among the onlookers laughing along with me, so I invited her to join me as my ministry team. Together, we continued laughing over the woman's leg for a few minutes, and then asked her to check to see if there was any improvement. She began to move her big toe, and her husband shouted out that she had not been able to do that.

We laughed some more and re-checked. She began to move all of her toes. Continuing to laugh, we removed a part of the brace that held her foot in place. Immediately, she began to move her entire foot. We then removed the piece of the brace holding her knee in place. She began flexing her leg at the knee, and now the entire group of onlookers was cheering and laughing as the miracle unfolded before their eyes.

At this point, the woman had to go into the restroom and remove her clothing to get the rest of the brace off. I sent the elderly ministry team assistant in with her with the instructions to continue to laugh while she was shedding the remaining piece of the brace. When the woman came out of the restroom, she was walking with a limp, but walking for the first time without any assistance. Her leg was coming back to life!

The next morning, she came to the meeting without her brace. After testifying before the entire conference of the events of the previous night, she ran around the auditorium holding her entire brace up over her head like a trophy as she and the crowd celebrated the miracle that had transpired.

At that point, I had everyone place their own hands on the parts of their bodies that needed healing, and instructed them to laugh over the ailments. Many were miraculously healed as the medicine of Heaven was released.

Increasing the Daily Dose

Joy is part of the fruit of the Spirit (see Gal. 5:22). Fruit, however, does not grow overnight—it must be cultivated over time. Similarly, the fruit of joy must be cultivated daily if we expect it in our lives. We must subject ourselves to the constant watering of the Holy Spirit, being continually filled with His presence in order for the fruit of joy to mature in our lives (see Eph. 5:18).

We have a part in cultivating the fruit as well. In Psalm 103, David declares, *"Praise the Lord, O my soul."* David was basically saying, "Soul, I know that you do not want to praise God right now, but you are not in charge of my life—I am. So, I will bless the Lord." Everything we do in the Kingdom is done by choice through our will. We love, forgive, serve, give, and praise God by choice, through faith, with the grace that God gives us to be able to do it.

Laughter, which is a manifestation of joy, is also cultivated by choice. Too many believers are waiting for God to supernaturally cause them to laugh or are waiting until they have a feeling of joy before they enter into their Kingdom right to laugh. We do not live by feelings; we live by faith. As believers, we are to live according to the core values of the Kingdom of God, not the present realities of our feelings or circumstances.

There are times when I do not feel like loving someone, but I do not live according to my feelings. No, I love because it is right to love, so I choose to love even though I do not feel like it. Those who become mature as believers are those who have learned to cultivate the fruit of the Spirit by daily choice—"I will." To that end, I schedule intentional times to cultivate the fruit. For example, I have a date night with my wife every week to ensure that we spend quality time together to cultivate our love.

It's the same way with the fruit of joy. I do not just laugh when I feel joyful or something funny is said. I often will laugh when I notice that I am not feeling very joyful. I have learned to laugh regularly and intentionally in order to cultivate the fruit of joy in my life.

I do this sometimes when I'm driving because there are many opportunities to cultivate joy when people cut me off or traffic lights do not seem to be in sync with my tight schedule. One day, while stopped at the fifth red light in a row, I turned the rearview mirror to myself and began to laugh with myself.

After a short time, I looked over at the car parked next to me where a woman apparently had been watching me laugh into my review mirror. She was laughing so hard watching me laugh that she had tears streaming down her cheeks. When the light turned green, I sped away, feeling much better about the next red light I would encounter, and happy that I had released a dose of Vitamin J to an unexpecting motorist.

I want to encourage you to continually cultivate the fruit of joy every day because it is the nutrient of Heaven that makes us and keeps us healthy and whole in every way.

In Jesus' last prayer for His disciples in John 17, He said that His reason for praying was so that they would have a full measure of His joy within them (see John 17:13). Of course, the size of Jesus' measure is unlimited, which means His desire for us is to have an unlimited measure of joy in our lives. His last prayer was to pass on a key to Kingdom life that would enable us to fulfill our supernatural destiny, living in wholeness and releasing wholeness everywhere we go to whomever we meet.

Joy is the medicine from Heaven provided to help us live full and well lives. It is God's nutritious heavenly fruit to overcome the effects of sin and death. It is important, then, to take our daily dose of joy in increasing measure to ensure that we are carrying His presence and power.

Impartation for Increase

I release the grace to live in new levels of joy, gladness, laughter, cheer, and merriment. May you find new and creative ways of expressing the joy of the Lord every day. May you experience increasing health, wholeness, and wellbeing as the medicine of Heaven saturates your mind, body, and soul.

Points to Ponder

1. What level of joy are you living in currently? How is your joy demonstrated practically?

2. How can you cultivate new levels of joy in your life?

Activation Activities

1. Count how many times per day you laugh. Record each time for a week and evaluate. Increase as needed.

2. Record the impact laughter had upon your spiritual, emotional, and physical wellbeing.

ENDNOTE

1. Berit Brogaard, "Effects of Laughter on the Human Brain," Livestrong.com, August 24, 2010, Stress Relief, The Brain's Reward System, accessed October 07, 2012, http://www.livestrong.com/article/170399-effects-of-laughter-on-the-human-brain.

THE HEALTH OF RECEIVING GOD'S LOVE
—CHAPTER 3—

...that Christ may dwell in your hearts through faith;
that you, being rooted and grounded in love, may be
able to comprehend with all the saints what is the
width and length and depth and height—to know the
love of Christ which passes knowledge; that you may be
filled with all the fullness of God (Eph. 3:17-19).

If we could sum up the Bible in one word, I think it would be love. God is love, and everything He does is motivated by love. Nothing marks a life like a personal encounter with God's love.

Nothing could be better for one's health—physically, spiritually, and emotionally—than the assurance of being truly loved. If you Google the effects of love, you will find countless articles and research about the effects of a mother's love, a spouse's love, a father's love, or the love of friends, even of pets, on a person's wellbeing, physical health, will to live, and so on.

So what are we to do if we lack one or many of the kinds of love that we need to feel whole and fulfilled? The answer lies in this next chapter, written by one who attests to a profound encounter with the love of God, the kind of experience that cannot be hidden, the kind that changes everything. Her current mission is to spill it out on everyone she meets, igniting their own passion for the Lord. So snuggle up to your loved one (or your cat) and read with anticipation. —P.S.

Love Heals Through a Dopamine Drip

by Deborah Stevens

LOVE—THE FOUNDATION OF HEALTH

Love is the foundation of our entire life and health. We were created in love, for love, and to be loved. Through love, we are made healthy in all areas of our lives.

Before we have been tenderly instructed to love, God has given us an invitation to receive His love: *"We love, because He first loved us"* (1 John 4:19 NAS).

THE PERCEPTION OF LOVE

We hear so many messages that influence our perception of love. We have spoken and unspoken messages that we have received through our families, the church, the media, music, etc. All of these varying sources and their mixed messages may have made hazy up our understanding of the true meaning of love.

We each develop our own vocabulary for love through what we've learned and heard about love. We have endless applications for the word itself and use it in so many different contexts. For instance, I recently saw a sign for *"Love's* Gas Station" as well as a clothing store called *"Love's* Apparel." We use it to proclaim with passionate expressions things like, "I *love* pizza," "I *love* her haircut," or, "I *love* to go on a vacation." We have all kinds of expressions and interpretations of love in our hearts that have been established and built upon from what we have heard, seen, and experienced through our lives. These messages may have contributed to our perceptions and we may also have become a little desensitized along the way, causing us to turn a deaf ear to discussions on love. Do you get excited when you hear a message or see a book about love? If not, why. Love is everything we are born for and are living for. The Kingdom of Heaven is released on earth as we release the wisdom of God's love.

Many of us had difficult and challenging perceptions of love that have resulted from abusive relationships that may have proclaimed love but did not display love for what it really is meant to be. My own perception of love regarding relationships had been distorted as a result of disappointments, betrayals, and verbal and emotional abuse. My perception of love needed to be overhauled and be healed and established by an encounter with God's true love. As a result of my experiences with "love," I stopped enjoying love stories and seeing people in love. I had disconnected and shut down this area in my life and disconnected myself from some aspects of love. Even though I had been in a church family for many years and had been serving in ministry a long time, I came to a realization that I was missing a depth of connection that I felt I had not really known or experienced. I was missing out on something that was available to me and was rightfully mine—the fullness of the Kingdom reality of the love of God. I had become desensitized, numb even, and I desperately wanted to feel and know love in every area of my life and to fervently, abundantly, wholly be able to love with everything within me. I just didn't know how to have that happen, and I hadn't encountered, experienced, developed, and understood what was available to me.

In fact, it's a total miracle for me to be associating myself with this topic and writing about love because, in some respects, I had difficulty in believing in some facets of love. I wasn't aware of how much I needed healing until I realized that I was walking through life void of the feelings of love, at least in certain areas of life. It affected me so much that I stopped going to weddings. Though I cared deeply about my friends and had a great honor for their decisions to get married, I didn't want to pretend to be someone I was not by trying to support love while feeling disconnected from it. I knew I needed God to reveal His love to me in a life-altering way so that I could be healed from the misconceptions I had experienced through significant people's expression of false love in my life. I was missing an element of health and wholeness that affected my body, soul, and spirit. I knew I needed this miracle in my heart; it was essential in order for me to fulfill God's call on my life to love.

To love is the call that God has asked of all of us. There are many messages to preach and much to do in cultivating and bringing about the Kingdom of Heaven on the earth as it is in Heaven, but the entire reason we do what we do must be rooted and grounded in love , and for the sake of love.

AN ENCOUNTER WITH LOVE, HIMSELF

I had a transforming encounter with the love of God that brought healing to my entire being. I think the best way to describe this deep encounter that I had was that it felt like I was being born again, all over again. I encountered God and His love like I never had before. It invaded all of my body, soul, and spirit, and it healed me to such a degree that I knew my life had been forever changed. I knew that this encounter was not something that the Lord was doing in just me as I had sensed that He was doing the same thing in His church as a whole.

One morning at church I experienced a really strong impression from the Holy Spirit and heard Him say, "My church is getting born again." I thought that was a strange thing to hear. After I heard Him say this to me, one of our pastors, whom I was standing next to, said in that very moment the exact words, that I had just heard. I knew God was up to something, and I was so glad to be a part of it. He is bringing us into wholeness and maturity to be all that He has designed our lives to be, in preparation for a beautiful wedding. I have been transformed through an extended encounter with love throughout this past year. Love changes everything! One encounter with God changes everything.

Love Is the Message

One morning as I was getting ready for work, I had a strong impression that I *had* to wear a t-shirt that had two little dogs holding a sign up that said "Love is the Message" written on the front of it. I usually dress professionally, and this was not exactly the kind of attire I wear to work, but it was a strong impression in my spirit, and I felt I needed to respond to what I was hearing. I went to get the shirt with this message on it, only to find it buried in the washing hamper. I didn't understand why I would feel the need to wear that, and it wasn't even clean. I couldn't shake the feeling, so I got dressed and thought I would stop at the store I bought it from and see if there was another one. They had one—and it was on sale and in my size! Of course I bought it and put on my "Love is the Message" shirt and off I went to work, excited to see what the day would bring.

I arrived at work heavily under the influence of the Holy Spirit by this time. One of my former staff and long-time friends, Faith Stromback, exclaimed, "Deborah! I can't believe you're wearing that shirt! Last night I had a dream of you, and I was with Jesus and basically what happened was, I asked Jesus, 'Why is there such an increase of God's presence at work?' And He replied, 'Because Deborah is spreading the love around.'" This presence of love was healing our staff from the inside out during this time.

At that point in my journey, I really didn't feel that I had done a great job in the area of showing, expressing or being loving to those in my sphere of influence. I was still in the process of getting healed. God is so kind to trust us, even while we are growing, and He is so intentional in encouraging us along the way and in saying, "Well done!" wherever we are in our journey. Even if we have only taken two steps, He is there pursuing us with love and encouraging us to keep going. There is so much pleasure and reward to enjoy in being obedient to the call to love.

One day, one of my friends, Iain Bradbeer, looked me in the eye and asked me a serious question. I knew by the expression on his face that Holy Spirit was about to say something through him. I had just finished speaking at a seminar and was feeling like my presentation wasn't done well. I was also a little intimidated about talking about this love message because of my own past inadequacies in my example of loving. We are all on an adventure; we make what we feel are mistakes along the way, and when we fall short of expressing love well, the perfect love of God is there to help us as we clean up our mess.

So my friend Iain asked me, "Deborah, if a house was on fire, and someone was in the house and going to die, would you drag them out by the hair if it meant you would be saving their life?"

I immediately replied, "Of course I would!"

He said, "Sometimes that's what the ferocious love of God looks like. These people's houses are burning down, and their lives are at stake. God has asked you to help them, and it might not feel really comfortable, but it's necessary." That word from God through Iain confirmed what God had been doing in and speaking to me. I knew I had to continue with telling people the testimony of the love message that had been burned in my heart even though I was still working on it happening in me, and that it wasn't the most popular message of the hour.

Though God's requests for us to *love* sound like commands, please know that they're coming from a loving Dad. He tells us to love for our benefit because it results in an increase of life and health in our own lives. When these commands are expressed over and over in His Word, it is with soft eyes and a heart full of fiery love that He says it. It's not from an angry, demanding God. It's with His deep, kind, fathering heart that He tells us the truth of what is needed to be healthy and to live a life of wholeness that takes us through to eternity.

I know we feel we have heard it all before, but something different is happening in our being awakened to love. Sometimes the awakening might feel like His hand lovingly dragging us by the hair out of the house we just set on fire so that our lives will be saved. Even our singed hair will be restored. He is trying to get our attention through calling us into a global love movement that will bring health in every area of His Bride as we are preparing for our wedding with our Bridegroom. We will answer the call, and we are going to be glorious and ready!

The Vision of the Dopamine Drip

This might sound a bit mystical, but it is my testimony of what happened to me. I have a lot of angelic and mystical encounters, life-changing both for me and for others when I share them. In January of 2012, I had a vision of an enormous IV bag in the sky. I asked Holy Spirit, "What is that IV bag for?" and "What is it filled with?" I heard Him say that it was filled with dopamine and that it was an IV love drip for the world. I had never seen or heard about anything like this before.

Since I wasn't familiar with dopamine, I did a little research on it, and what I discovered was extremely interesting. It turns out that dopamine is significant for a number of reasons. I'm not an expert on this, so please don't get stuck on the details. It wasn't my idea for the bag to be filled with dopamine; through seeing the benefits of dopamine, I could see God had a strategic and fun plan. I am only going to point out a few of dopamine's benefits.

I discovered that dopamine is a hormone and neurotransmitter. It can be prescribed by doctors, to stimulate, and it has been used to improve the firing of connectors (specifically nerve cell synapses) in our body. When something has stopped them from working correctly, they need help to increase communication on their own again. These connections are needed in order to have emotional and physical health. Dopamine helps to send a signal to our cells, which produces good feelings in us. A disturbance of dopamine regulation and the disconnection of firing between connectors results in a person's no longer being able to respond emotionally as well as disrupting parts of our system physically. So dopamine can help heal our ability to connect and respond emotionally.

I was in awe how it could be one of the ways used to bring about healing. There are so many other benefits of dopamine; it's really a miracle chemical, and it naturally occurs in our body. God is the Creator of all things, even chemicals. He created the chemical dopamine in our body on purpose to fulfill certain needs in our system. If the world is getting a dopamine drip as I saw in the vision, then there is a reconnection about to happen for the planet to respond to love and to be connected to God and to each other. Great idea! Hook us up, Lord! Those who desire this connection are about to be inoculated with love through a dopamine drip.

Though this vision seems metaphorical, the feelings and metamorphosis that come with the infusion of this chemical are not. They actually *feel* like the dopamine you feel coursing through your body when you fall in love with someone. It would be the same kind of experience as if you had a broken bone, and it was healed miraculously. There is actually something that happens in your physical body that is real.

After seeing the vision of the dopamine drip, I realized I was continually and intensely feeling something in my body that was reminiscent of the feelings I knew from being in love. It had started happening to me; the dopamine drip had been hooked up to me! I could actually feel the chemical in my body. I have never taken cocaine, but from what I have read about dopamine, it is compared to the good feelings that come with cocaine. Just as someone takes cocaine and feels something, I was feeling dopamine in my system; only I never put it in there! I started waking in the night hours with feelings of being so deeply in love with God. I spent hours upon hours worshiping; almost all my waking hours apart from working and sleeping were spent studying and worshiping. I couldn't get enough of Him. Sound familiar? When you are in love, you just want to forsake everything and be with the one you love. The intensity of this encounter with love has not stopped. It has altered my life, my longings, and desires, it has completely changed me. There are many areas of my life that are transformed, but the two most dramatic ones have to do with connection and believing in love.

This intense time of love brought so much healing to my life. I had for 14 years not been able to really connect with people in the depth that I hoped for and felt I should. God had healed my ability to connect in love. As a matter of fact, I started shocking people by the connection that I was making with them. They had never experienced me in this way. My heart became so tender and in love with everyone around me. Yes! *In love*, not just love. I felt (and still feel) in love with everyone. A burning in my heart along with a desire to pour out love on people has been ignited.

As I spent time interacting with the love of God through drawing close to Him in worship and spending time in His Word, God began to draw close to me. I had heard Heidi Baker speak of this love and prayed that I would feel and know what she had expressed when I heard her speak. I began to feel and know an intimacy with His heart that I had always longed for. His love healed my love so deeply that a dramatic shift happened in my life. Where I had had a difficult time in believing in love, *now* I could believe in love. I felt that this dopamine chemical was released in my body and that it resulted in my feeling and even more importantly, knowing love in deeper ways than ever before. I had found myself with a new and deep love for those around me.

The ability to prove being healed by love seems intangible in some ways as love is not measurable, nor is it easily described, much like our limitless God, who is neither measurable nor easily described. But He is God, and He is love and He is healer. I know I have been healed and have been transformed like a caterpillar, that is reborn into a butterfly. It's given me wings to fly and be who I was created to be. There is a defined and definite metamorphosis that has taken place. I have feelings and actions that I wasn't able to have for years.

I know it seems a little out of the norm, the details of this vision I had of a dopamine drip, but God is creative and often mystical in how He speaks to us and ministers to each of us in a language we individually can understand. We all know God is healer, but we don't always know *how* He is going to heal. I was so encouraged by this vision and how practical it was and that He would show me by example one of the ways He was going to heal us. And his kindness in doing this in mystical language which I personally related to and enjoy so much. He showed me even through that vision, how He knows me, and brought healing through a way that personally speaks to me

"Dripping" on Others

Recently, I went to Starbucks to get a coffee, and when I went to order, I asked them for a dopamine! I had meant to ask for a "doppio," but "dopamine with steamed brevé, please" came out of my mouth. I was as shocked at my statement as they were. This happened to me three separate times when ordering at various Starbucks cafés. Every time it happened, the staff started laughing so hard, as did the people standing in line behind me. One particular time the girl who took my order was laughing so hard that she couldn't even write on my cup and had to hand it to someone else. She said, "You know, I think I really need one of those, too!"

The other girl working with her said, "I think that is what is wrong with me: I need some dopamine." Twice the people behind me asked for what I was having and fully meant it. One time a nice Asian lady, who did not speak a lot of English, asked for *three* of what I was having! God has a beautiful plan for our love lives, so to speak.

This experience of love with God and with the dopamine drip completely changed me. I was reconnected with people through my emotional and spiritual wiring being overhauled. My connections—including feelings of love—to those I was in relationship with were reset and rebuilt. I felt like I had been waiting for this fullness of love my whole life. It was just that powerful. I felt like I was deeply in love with the *first love* kind of love, and that knowing and force of love hasn't stopped.

I began to pray for people to receive their *first love* connection with God again—and to have their love connection in all areas of their lives reconnected. Though I expected my prayers to work, it was still such a surprise at the intensity of it really igniting in people. The people I was praying for were having intense healing encounters in their love lives with God and with others. The testimonies began to come in. I started to hear of how their lives had been changed by this reconnection of love in them after I had prayed for them.

This past year I have heard such an exponential increase of messages about love. God is answering the desires of our hearts to be healed and to fully know and experience love. This is His design and desire for us as well. Here are a few of those testimonies about how it only takes one encounter of love from God in order to have our misconceptions and paradigms of love completely healed and restored.

Testimony I—Santiago

My life is changed. You are the person God used to bring the revelation of God's love in my life. I became a different man within four days of this encounter with God's love through you. My testimony is strong and the best thing that happened to me is that this love of God broke every religious structure in me. It let me enter into a new dimension with God. Now I can understand and start to live with everything that my Papa God has said is mine and to know I am His, that He lives inside of me, around me, and through me. (My identity in Him was revealed.) My life was healed and liberated by God's love, and through this I am now releasing the presence of God into places and people. I am now, through His love, bringing healing and liberation to others.

Testimony 2—Juan

My name is Juan; I'm 18. Ten years ago, I was abused many times by a family friend. I've always been shy, but after that situation, I couldn't talk with other boys of my age. I wouldn't even receive a hug from my daddy. I couldn't take my shirt off when going swimming in a pool because I felt unprotected. I was thinking about suicide because of how sad I was, and then God used a man I met named Martin who became a very close friend. Martin showed so much love to me. He would hug me, pray with me, and stay with me as much time as was necessary. I was going to commit suicide because of the pain I was in, but I'm still here, and it's because of love. Jesus' love for me through this man made me someone new. Love gave me hope and a desire that's stronger than ever to worship

God. During this time of healing, I ran into this abuser on the bus. I came home really sad, angry, and nervous. I met Deborah on a missions trip in Argentina, and she spoke with me about love. I got online and I talked to Deborah. She is someone who always makes me feel loved and special. She listened to the situation, gave me advice about it, and expressed how much she cares for me and how much God loves me. With that I was encouraged, and I felt good and strong again. I was feeling the love that I knew was mine, and it brought confidence and it gave me strength to run to God's arms so I could rest in Him and be healed. I'm alive, and I'm who I am today because of love. Because of Jesus' love and through this man who helped me and through Deborah, I am now helping kids from the orphanage push through these situations as I've been through it, too. I must say I see how love is changing those kids as well and how they are being completely healed by love. I can trust people, and I'm not afraid anymore.

Testimony 3—Sarah

Feeling First Love

For as long as I can remember, I have loved the Lord. My parents were pastors who raised me in the church and introduced me to the Lord at a very young age. I remember being about five years old when I gave my heart to the Lord and have ever since walked with and lived for Him. Though I've always loved the Lord, I didn't realize that I had rarely felt the actual feeling of first love. I had memorable experiences and encounters and I had certainly felt love for the Lord to a degree. However, the depth of the feeling of first love had grown dull.

Again, I wasn't fully aware of this until after a staff meeting one day. We were all standing in line, waiting for prayer and impartation from a guest speaker and his team (of which Deborah was a part). I began to feel my heart being pricked by the Lord in a deep way, and by the time I received prayer by the team and Deborah, I felt completely overwhelmed by the love of God and my desire to love Him in return. This experience lasted several hours after the staff meeting and prayer time had ended, and it took me all that time to discover what I was really feeling and what was really happening on the inside of me. It felt like a brand new love and when I recognized what God was doing in me, in tears from the overwhelming depth of what I was feeling, I turned to Deborah and said, "I feel like I found first love again. I had always hoped I would, but didn't know that it would happen."

LOVE EVERLASTING

I am on a mission, and I'm not exactly sure how to complete it yet, but I want to find a way to maintain the "Honeymoon Period" in our love lives with God and with each other. I know it's possible that we would be able to fully love with all our heart, mind, soul, and strength, all of the time, for the rest of our lives. He wouldn't have asked this of us unless He had enabled us to do it.

We are a bride preparing for her bridegroom. Love does not back off and lessen as the wedding date draws near. It is relentless and pursuing. Love is the most important word that surrounds a bride, a groom, and the wedding. It's time for love. It's natural, healthy, and normal for a bride to be in love, to feel love, and be love as she prepares for her wedding day. What's not natural is for her to be devoid of love, including the emotion and feelings of love.

We are daily and forever meant to be in love and live a life of love that is passionate. It's normal for us to display our affection for God and for one another. He desires to lavish tender, kind, strong, fierce, burning, fiery, relentless, passionate, persevering, courageous, extravagant, whole-hearted, loyal, longing, jealous, love toward and on us. He desires for us to be that same kind of lover as He is. He desires for us to be fully in love with Him and with each other and with ourselves. Not to just love but to be in love.

My life has been healed and completely changed by God's love. My hope and prayer for us all is that we would all on a global scale encounter the love of God in practical and manifest ways in our body, soul, and spirit, and then through the fullness of His love in us, that we would spread the love of God throughout this planet.

Dopamine anyone? (I may have overdosed on it while writing this.)

And may our love story into eternity be: "And they lived happily ever after in love."

PHYSICAL HEALTH
—CHAPTER 4—

Or do you not know that your body is the temple of the Holy Spirit who is in you, whom you have from God, and you are not your own? (1 Cor. 6:19)

What a funny mentality the Church has had over the centuries regarding our bodies. So many extremes exist, from those who erroneously harm themselves thinking to overcome their "lower nature," to those who behave as if this temporary "house" were their eternal castle. Neither extreme is healthy. While we can add nothing to our salvation by harming ourselves, and our bodies are not in themselves evil, our bodies *can* be exacting usurpers of authority if we allow them to dictate our lives and if we indulge their every whim or endlessly pamper them.

Somehow health lies in between the extremes. Let's face it; we need our bodies to remain on this earth—at least, above ground. A healthy attitude to our bodies is neither to neglect nor to idolize them, but to treat them with respect because they are the house where God dwells on this earth. They are the earthen containers that carry Him. What I see around me is that the effect of spiritual health manifests somehow in our bodies, whether it be in our countenance or in our physical health. Many times it seems to result in our return to our original weight or in taking good care of ourselves. I chose the author for the next chapter because he not only pursues divine healing, but also has a testimony of physical transformation by natural means. We can all learn from his story. (This chapter will make you want to drop that doughnut and grab a carrot stick.)—P.S.

Walking in God's Best with Our Health

by Chris Gore

I love miracles, and since I saw my first miracle through my hands in April 2005, it has been my absolute joy to see many thousands of miracles. I simply love to see Jesus get what He paid for. I have seen many amazing healings and many wonderful creative miracles.

I love to see the looks on people's faces when they have just received a powerful touch from God. I love to see people who have lived in torment for many years set free by the power of the cross. The longest condition that I saw someone set free from lasted over 70 years. I am so compelled to operate and demonstrate the love of Jesus to the people to whom I have the joy to minster. As a pastor at Bethel Church, I have the privilege of traveling to many cities and nations each year and partnering with Heaven to see Jesus' Kingdom come on earth and see Him get His full reward.

However, as wonderful and as fun as miracles are, I believe that miracles are not God's best for a person's life. Let me explain. Over the past few years in walking out my own journey into a lifestyle of miracles, I have battled with my own health issues that I have not seen miraculously healed—well, not miraculously in the sense that you may think of miraculous.

Our bodies are an intricate design by an incredible Designer. Our bodies are created to operate in an efficient manner and repair themselves, but what they need to do this is correct nutrition and care. I have been on a journey to discover how our bodies function and how they are designed to heal themselves when required. God's best for our lives is to walk in divine health, but I came to a point where I had to ask myself why we are not seeing many walk in God's best for their lives.

In June 2010, I went to the doctor for an annual health check-up, thinking that I was in pretty good shape. I got the report back a few days later that my blood sugar level was too high, and I was diagnosed with pre-stage diabetes. This was a real shock, so I booked myself in to see a doctor who specialized in a holistic approach to health through nutrition. I was asked to record everything that I ate in a week's window and was pretty impressed with what I thought was a good, balanced diet.

I went back to see my doctor, and my report revealed that most of the items that I had been eating contained little or zero nutrition, and in most cases simply were poor food choices. She asked me about my health and other areas that were of concern to me. I explained that I had suffered severe asthma for over 38 years, and on several occasions as a child, I was admitted to hospital and did not display a lot of promise on getting through the night.

I was clearly out of shape and eating the wrong food. I also explained to the doctor that seasons of overbearing discouragement would flood over me, which was strange, as I was in the midst of seeing the most incredible miracles in people's lives on a daily basis. I explained that it was like a shadow that I could see coming and nothing that I did would make it stop, and once it was on me, nothing I did could make it leave (I call it *brain fog*). It seemed like it would come and go as it chose, and I had absolutely no control over it. It would leave me with incredible fatigue and was wearing on my life and on the life of my family.[1]

The doctor made notes, and I was sent off for some simple testing. A week or so later, at a follow-up appointment, I was told that I have a severe allergy to gluten, a protein found in wheat, oats, and rye. My report showed that my allergy was so high (even off the chart) that I needed to simply stop all intake of gluten.

What was there to lose? I removed myself from all gluten to see what might happen. This was an educational process in itself as gluten is hidden in so many foods. The results were simply outstanding. To my shock, the clouds of discouragement (brain fog) left immediately. The clouds simply don't come any longer. The days are brighter, and my life is totally changed. My wife described it as the difference between night and day.

Something else happened. At the time of writing this chapter in July 2012, it has now been two years since I have needed to use my asthma inhaler. Overnight, my asthma, which I have suffered with for over 38 years, was gone. I have seen so many doctors and specialists over the years and taken so many trips to emergency care and hospitals, yet all the care I received was treating the symptom, not the issue. Never had anyone suggested to me that what I ate could be a cause for the torment in my lungs.

Before taking myself off gluten, I could not go a day without once or twice needing medication and could rarely sleep through the night without waking gasping for breath. I was unable to run for any distance without needing an inhaler, but since getting off gluten, I can easily run for six miles without needing to stop. I get to travel the world, and, whereas before I would never be anywhere without an inhaler in my pocket, now I would not even know where to find one if I needed it. As I write this, I celebrate today two years asthma free.

I was already on a journey to lose weight; at the time of seeing the doctor, I had lost 20 pounds, and since that time, I have lost a total of 45 pounds. Today, I weigh the least that I have in my adult life. I simply feel so much better. I have more energy, more joy, and an even happier marriage. The one consistent comment that I have received is that I look ten years younger, and I also certainly feel like it.

As I write about my personal journey into health, I want to stress that while I love to eat well, what I eat and what I drink are not my redeemer and savior; the Lord Jesus Christ is. Eating healthfully and treating my body well is good stewardship; it's a way that I can worship God.

Knowledge Was the Key

Have you ever realized that it's not the truth that sets us free; it's the knowledge of the truth that sets us free? If it was just the truth, we would all be free and healthy. So I went on a journey to seek knowledge and educate myself. I so love seeing miracles, but I want to see people get free from sickness and *stay* free from sickness. (I have a teaching called "Authority to Stay Free from Sickness," which addresses this issue in greater depth, also from a spiritual side).

I took to the books to educate myself on how I might walk in divine health. While what I discovered was so simplistic, I was still so shocked to see how I was destroying my own body by poor choices. The American diet, which would be similar to that of many other countries, has become a fast and convenient diet with little or zero nutrition. We are generally a society that lives to eat, not eats to live. We have become a society that has an addiction to sugar, and because of it we are becoming more obese by the day.

Today the average American person consumes over 150 pounds (66 kilograms) of sugar per year; that's around 50 teaspoons per day. We wonder why we have a battle with the bulge; it's our poor food choices. Diabetes is extremely prevalent, and researchers are seeking the next medicine to treat the symptoms of this disease, but what needs to be addressed is the root of the problem—our diet, our waistline, and our lifestyles.

Please hear my heart in this. This is not to judge the obese or to instill fear into anyone. In fact, when I see people who are overweight or obese, I silently release grace and peace into their situation and pray that their eyes would be opened to seeing God's best for their health. My hope in writing this chapter is that you would be prompted to begin to look at what you eat, so that we can all walk in God's best for our lives. I was in the overweight range, and while I have lost 45 pounds, to remain in the ideal healthy weight range still requires hard work and daily dedication.

Personally I don't like diets. I have seen many diets come and go and seen people lose weight on a diet but have no idea how to eat for lifestyle; within a short time after reaching their goal weight, they pack the pounds back on. Lifestyle eating is a daily choice. People need to educate themselves as to what they should eat and what should be minimized or totally avoided.

I know that this is not a revelation to many people, so what many have done is to lower their intake of obvious refined sugar to help themselves lose weight and have replaced it with artificial sweeteners, which are causing all manner of other issues. It's not just a matter of losing weight; it's a matter of ensuring that what we are consuming is good for our bodies.

Some sugar substitutes, such as aspartame, are promoted to us on the basis that they contain few or no calories. But there is much research that you can do for yourself that points to the fact that aspartame can cause cancer and many other serious health issues; in fact, one report that I researched shows that the use of aspartame showed over 92 different health side effects, yet today aspartame is used widely in many processed foods, baked goods, powered drink mixes, soft drinks, breath mints, instant breakfasts, sugar free chewing gum, candy, canned foods, jams, dairy products and many other foods and beverages.[2]

There are some more healthy options that we can choose from. I personally use NuStevia, which is natural and taken from a plant extract, and it contains no calories or aspartame.

We have become so obsessed with sugar and/or high-fructose corn syrup (HFCS). Our excessive intake of sugar and/or HFCS and a sedentary lifestyle are considered to be at least partly responsible for the diabetes epidemic that we are seeing in the world today. Diabetes today is classed as the silent killer and now ranks as the seventh leading cause of death by disease in America.[3] The World Health Organization now estimates that by 2030, the number of people with diabetes worldwide will double.[4] Simply put, that number could reach as high as 360 million people within the next 18 years. Today, approximately 10 percent of Americans over 20 have diabetes. So 24 million Americans suffer from diabetes, and what is more alarming is that a fourth of them do not know that they have it.[5]

Childhood diabetes is growing at a staggering rate, and researchers at the Centers for Disease and Control Prevention (CDC) have made the prediction that without making changes to the way we eat and exercise, one in three children born in the US are likely to develop Type 2 diabetes at some point in their lives.[6]

I realized that I needed to change my lifestyle and eating habits. Trust me, I am not the perfect role model, but things have dramatically changed in my life over the past three years. The first thing that I eliminated from my life was soda—*all* soda, including diet soda, which is full of artificial sweeteners. I have now gone three years without having a soda.

The next thing that I eliminated was high fructose corn syrup (HFCS), then almost all processed foods, which HFCS is heavily used in, and more recently, the elimination of as much sugar out of my diet as I possibly can. I was recently on a ministry trip, and there was a gift basket of food in my hotel. I normally would have enjoyed the treats without much of a thought. I sat down to enjoy and looked on the back of the packets and counted over one pound of sugar (500 grams) in the few treats that were in my room. Out of the entire basket, I enjoyed some special cheeses (my weakness) and some nuts, and the bottled water. The rest went in the trash.

I am convinced that one of the main keys to better health is nutrition. Not just better nutrition, but to stop eating items that are full of ingredients that are killing us slowly. I try to eat fresh, rather than processed, and I have reduced my red meat intake immensely. Please understand—this is another incredible weakness for me. I would be happy to live on just red meat and lots of it! When I do eat red meat, I try to find grass fed meat, as opposed to corn or grain fed meat. I have reduced my dairy intake, significantly reduced my sugar intake, and totally eliminated high fructose corn syrup.

Weight Loss

Battling or preventing diabetes with weight loss through a combination of right eating and exercise could be one of the best things that you could do for your body. Control of your weight is an incredibly powerful key to not only the management but the prevention of diabetes. Type 2 diabetes is linked directly to obesity and foods that are rich in sugars, refined carbohydrates, and fats.

The larger our waist gets, the greater chances we have of getting Type 2 diabetes. A male with a waistline of 34 to 36 inches (not your beltline, but around the middle of your waist) has increased his chance of getting diabetes by twice and the chances of diabetes only exponentially go up from there as the waistline increases beyond 36 inches.[7]

Just as important, if not more so, is the need for exercise. Because of our jobs, many have become so busy, and in many cases inactive, that exercise is no longer a part of their lives. The many benefits of exercise include reducing the risk of dying prematurely or developing diabetes or high blood pressure, depression, anxiety, or heart disease. Exercise helps us to control weight and maintain healthy bones, muscles, and joints. It promotes better psychological wellbeing.

I could address each one of these as separate items, but I wanted to address one in particular: how exercise can help prevent or control diabetes and heart disease.

Please don't stop reading here because you don't have Type 2 diabetes or pre-diabetes. The benefits of fitness in preventing diabetes apply to everyone.

Your heart is a muscle—one of the most critical muscles in your body because it controls the flow of blood around your system. It's like a pumping station—the right side bringing in blood from your body and pumping it to your lungs, and the left side bringing in blood from the lungs and pumping it to the rest of your body.

Continuous and sustained exercise can help to condition the heart and lungs. When you exercise, you breathe faster, and your heart pumps more blood throughout your body. Your blood provides your body with oxygen and important nutrients, while at the same time carrying harmful waste products out of your body. Regular physical activity can help to reduce the risk of heart disease, the leading cause of death throughout the world.[8] The need for exercise cannot be stressed enough.

Aerobic exercises like walking, swimming, or cycling can help you lose weight, improve your heart health, and control your blood sugar better. I personally love to cycle. We have a river in Redding with a paved track around it. I can walk the 5.7-mile track in 75 minutes or bike it twice in 60 minutes.

Resistance exercise—strength training—has shown to have a profound impact on helping to prevent or to manage diabetes. For people with Type 2 diabetes, exercising regularly can even eliminate the need for constant medication, particularly when it's accompanied with a lifestyle of healthy eating. Again, please consult your doctor, who, I'm sure, will be very happy to assist you in adjusting medication as you make healthy lifestyle choices.

While I love to see the power of Heaven invade people's lives and see disease bow its knee to Jesus miraculously, I do believe in taking responsibility for our bodies and looking after them the best that we can, while still believing in God for the impossible. A lady came to me recently who had advanced cancer and was not looking good at all. I got talking to her and ministered the love of God to her. She really was looking very glum. She happened to mention to me that she juices several times per day in an effort to beat cancer. I said, "That's awesome. I also love to juice."

Her countenance changed, and she smiled and said, "You juice, yourself?"

I said, "Yes, I love to drink kale juice and lots of green juice, and if I was in your position, I would be doing exactly what you are doing." She told me that she had been told that by juicing, she was not trusting God and that she lacked faith.

I said, "God's grace is opposed to *earning*, but it's not opposed to *effort*."

ZACCHAEUS VS. THE RICH YOUNG RULER

I have a message that I love to share, and it is the difference between the story of the rich young ruler in Luke 18:18-23 and the story of Zacchaeus in Luke 19:1-10. One point that I would love to bring out is that the rich young ruler tried to earn salvation. Religion is like that—it's cruel. There is always one more thing that you must do, yet the rich young ruler approached Jesus as a teacher of the law, so Jesus addressed him with the law. He tried to earn salvation by his good works. That day the rich young ruler left saddened. Yet when we look at the story of Zacchaeus, we see that, while he did not try to earn salvation, he did seek to see who Jesus was (see Luke 19:3), but because of the crowd and because he was short, he ran ahead of the crowd and climbed the sycamore tree to see Jesus as He was going to pass that way.

I shared these two stories with the precious lady standing in front of me and said that while the rich young man tried to earn what he wanted and Zacchaeus did not, Zacchaeus still needed to climb the tree. See, many times people think that we need to do nothing. But God's grace and our faith are a powerful combination. Faith requires an action, and many times that action is our effort out of our belief in the nature of God.

There is nothing wrong with making an effort to get well and to look after our bodies. It's good stewardship. God gave us these incredible bodies with an expectation that we would look after them well with good nutrients and exercise.

With tears in her eyes and a smile on her face, the lady said, "So it's OK for me to believe God and also juice?"

I said, "Of course it is." There is something really powerful about believing God. I saw something lift off her that day, and she broke out laughing and smiling. I was now able to minister to her, and she was in a place to really receive the release of Heaven into her body.

If you look at the miracles in the Bible, you will notice that often an act or effort was required to walk into the miracle that the person was seeking. I have seen so many miracles, including diabetes and cancer healed, and it breaks my heart when—after I see the invasion of Heaven into a person's body and see diabetes healed for them—they see it as a license to default to a life of eating ice cream, soda, and doughnuts. Six or twelve months down the track, they are more overweight than before they were healed, and they wonder why they are dealing with diabetes or the same sickness again.

Partnering with Peace

Repeat this: "I won't partner with fear." I believe that one of the most important things that we can do is to partner with peace. I love the story of the woman with the issue of blood in Mark 5:25-34. First off, there was still an effort required for her to receive a miracle; she still needed to push through the crowd to touch the hem of His garment.

The Bible tells us that the woman with the issue of blood had spent all that she had on many physicians over 12 years and still had the issue; in fact, it grew worse. She pushed through the crowd to touch the hem of Jesus' garment, and we are told that Jesus knew that power had left Him when the woman touched Jesus, and she was healed that moment. Then Jesus turned and said, "Who touched my clothes?" The woman, with fear and trembling, knowing what had just happened to her, came and fell down before Jesus and confessed the whole truth. Jesus said to her, "Daughter, your faith has made you well; go in peace and be healed of your affliction."

The phrase "go in peace," which appears a number of times in the Scripture—like in Acts 16:36, where the keeper of the prison said to Paul, *"Now therefore depart, and go in peace"*—literally means to "go in peace," like what you might say as a farewell as you go. In the original language, the word "in" within this phrase "go in peace" is *en,* which means "in."

But with the woman with the issue of blood, the word "in" within the phrase "go in peace" in Mark 5:34 is not *en* but *es,* which actually means, "go *into* peace." So it's not "go in peace;" it's "go into peace."

Jesus was saying to go into *shalom,* step into *shalom* like you would step into a house, the realm of *shalom.* Not only did the woman receive healing, she received wholeness. What Jesus was really saying is "go into peace and be healed," yet we see in Mark 5:29 that she was already healed. But in the original language, the phrase "go in (*es*) peace and be healed" actually means to "go into peace and continue to be well" or "go into peace and continue to maintain your health."

Right here Jesus is telling us the key to divine health. I believe that Jesus is suggesting that the root issue of the woman with the issue of blood was that what she was suffering was caused from a lack of peace. Yet the woman was just healed when she encountered the answer (Jesus); the root cause was addressed secondarily.

I dream of the Body of Christ being so aware of the answer that when we encounter sickness and disease, it would simply be one touch or one word that drives it away. I dream that what the Church would carry would be enough to see torment broken over lives without the needless searching for the why. The answer—Jesus—dwarfs any issue that we would ever encounter.

I have seen people healed of disease, but because they have not addressed the root cause of it, though they are healed, they do not step into peace, and in some cases within a matter of time, they walk back into their condition. Hence, I have started to a run a class at Bethel's Healing Rooms, after our guests have been ministered to, called "Walking in God's Best for Our Health."

So many conditions of sickness are caused by stress and lack of peace. People are stressed out, and we wonder why our blood pressure is soaring and other conditions are wrong in our bodies. We are not walking in peace and are letting our hearts be troubled. I'm learning to walk in a mindset of not letting my heart be troubled. We are each bombarded daily with the issues of life, and we let our hearts get troubled, and that is creating huge issues within our bodies. Jesus is literally telling the woman to "go into peace" and "continue to be well."

Practice walking in a mindset of saying, "Let not my heart be troubled." Trust me, I am still working on this. Just today I received terrible service at a government organization that so frustrated me, I felt my heart pressure going through the roof; it continued for 30 minutes after I had left until I reminded myself, "Let not my heart be troubled." I said it out loud and made the conscious decision to let the situation go.

Jesus just gave the woman who was healed of the issue of blood not only the secret of healing, but also the secret of walking in divine health. Divine health is more important than divine healing. I love to see the power of God invade into people's lives, but I long to see the day when people learn to walk in divine health and there is no one left to heal.

Many have the mentality that, "If I get sick, then I will just believe in divine healing." I think that there is a higher standard, and that is to believe for divine health. Yes, if you do get sick, then believe God for divine healing.

The enemy wants to create havoc in your emotions, and he wants you to lose your peace. Why? Because the enemy cannot manage a peaceful Christian, because the devil himself has no peace. Step into *shalom* peace. Step into God's best for your life and for your health. Keep your eyes on Jesus, the author and the finisher of your faith.

CONCLUSION

Christ has redeemed us from the curse of the law, having become a curse for us... (Galatians 3:13).

Galatians 3:13 tells us that Jesus was sent to redeem us from every curse that came upon creation with the fall of Adam. He has redeemed us from sickness, pain, sorrow, depression, poverty, and even death. The world may know Him as the Creator, but we have the joy of knowing Him also as the Redeemer. The work of creation cannot save us. His work of redemption can and has. When we go to Jesus, the sent one who came to redeem us with the price of blood, and we rest in the victory of the cross, we will receive the miracle that we need.

We will have greater health when we trust Him as the Redeemer than those who trust in creation. I love to eat well and exercise and take care of my body, but my trust is not in what I eat or drink; my trust is in the Redeemer Jesus Christ, who is my Healer, Provider, Deliverer, and Savior.

CLOSING PRAYER

I trust that I have spurred you on to choosing health and believing God to a new level for walking in divine health. Would you please pray this out loud with me?

Father, I thank you that you created me and I am your masterpiece. I thank you that the word of God says that I was created in your image and that you are not sick. So I thank you that I can come with absolute confidence that sickness is not from you and any sickness in my life is not your plan and therefore has *no place in my body. Jesus, I receive what you paid for my life, and I put my trust in you as the Redeemer because you paid for my personal full victory at the cross. I thank you that I am a new creation in Christ. I pray that you will give me greater revelation of not just who I am in Christ but who you are in me. I ask that I would receive greater revelation of my identity and my inheritance. I receive your best for my health and thank you that your best is for me to be **healthy, whole, restored and walking in divine health.***

ENDNOTES

1. Please note that I am not a doctor, and I am not making a medical diagnosis on your situation; I am not qualified to suggest what might be wrong with you. I am simply opening my life to share my journey. By no means is this chapter comprehensive on each of the topics I cover; I am just touching each one in brief and trusting that you are prompted to do further research yourself. In addition, please follow the advice of your health care professional, and make sure that you consult him or her before making lifestyle changes or exercise changes in your life. I have found that doctors love working with you more when they see that you are taking a proactive approach to your health. In addition to talking to your physician, choose to believe God—the Master Physician (see Luke 1:37 NLT).

2. Janet Star Hull, "Aspartame Side Effects," Sweetpoison. com, 2002, accessed October 07, 2012, http://www. sweetpoison.com/aspartame-side-effects.html.

3. "World Life Expectancy Map," World Life Expectancy, accessed October 07, 2012, http://www.worldlife expectancy.com.

4. "Diabetes," WHO, September 2012, accessed October 07, 2012, http://www.who.int/mediacentre/factsheets/fs312/en.

5. Number of Americans with Diabetes Projected to Double or Triple by 2050," Centers for Disease Control, October 22, 2011, accessed October 07, 2012, http://www.cdc.gov/media/pressrel/2010/r101022.html.

6. Ibid.

7. Dr. Don Colbert, *The New Bible Cure for Diabetes* (Lake Mary, FL: Siloam, 2009), 61.

8. The World Health Report, "Reducing Risks, Promoting Healthy Life," WHO, 2002, accessed October 07, 2012, http://www.who.int/whr/2002/en.

FAMILY HEALTH

—CHAPTER 5—

Now, therefore, you are no longer strangers and foreigners, but fellow citizens with the saints and members of the household of God, having been built on the foundation of the apostles and prophets, Jesus Christ Himself being the chief cornerstone, in whom the whole building, being fitted together, grows into a holy temple in the Lord, in whom you also are being built together for a dwelling place of God in the Spirit (Eph. 2:19-22).

I knew I had the right person to write about family health. His stories of his New York childhood home (with grandparents on one floor, an aunt and her family on another and his own family on a third) charm listeners and evoke nostalgia for what we all long for: a warm and loving family. Having had that and then carried it on with his wife and children, the author of this chapter passes on his prescription for a healthy family life and for extending that blessing way beyond genetics.

I don't know anything that spells health for a nation like whole and loving families. Family represents God's heart and values possibly more than anything. With the family under siege in our day, we believers have the opportunity to show to the world what Kingdom living can really be. And we possess a hope that others without Christ rarely do: the hope of reconciliation. That starts with God. Once reconciled to Him, we can pull on His grace to see our families healed. I heard a story just last week of a woman on the brink of divorce celebrating the restoration of her family as her husband overnight fell in love with the Lord and changed. Read this chapter with hope (and remember to phone your grandmother). —P.S.

Family Secret

by Matthew DiMarco

When asked how it was that he knew so many people, my dad's reply was, "Make everyone feel like family." By my dad's actions, what he meant was, *treat everyone who comes into your life just like you would treat family*. This philosophy is one of the simplest yet most profound truths that God has used to shape my life, my family, and our approach to relationships.

FAMILY—MULTIPLIED LOVE

So, what does a healthy family look like? What does a healthy family do? One key to healthy family is taking care of each other. A healthy family really, honestly cares for each other and for other people besides themselves. There have been many times when my wife, Trish, and I found out that young college-age friends of my son Jordan and my daughter Emily were eating Top Ramen because they had to make sure their bills were paid. Our response to that was, "No, you are going to come over to the house, and we are going to feed you. Oh yeah, and bring your laundry because we have a washer and dryer you can use, too." The laundry is important for obvious reasons, but the food thing is so big in our family. With a last name like DiMarco, eating is not just something we do; it is part of who we are. It is one of the most social, relationship-building things we can engage in.

I remember when my now daughter-in-law, Kristene, had dinner at the house for the first time. While sitting and eating, she realized how long it had been since she had sat around a table in a relaxed setting, eating good food, spending time for no other reason but to rest and hang out and receive love in a way that we sometimes forget in our fast-paced, make-it-quick lives. Since then she has described how that experience felt like warm love, like family.

We have had as few as one and as many as 80 people in our 1,850-square-foot house in Redding, California, at any given time. Usually the number falls between 6 and 10, but one time we unexpectedly had 22 people over the course of 30 minutes show up around dinner time. I had already been cooking the tomato sauce and meatballs for a good part of the afternoon and had about two pounds of pasta cooked and ready to go when it struck me that we didn't have enough food for everyone. Suddenly my spirit began to smile as I heard, "I have more than enough for 22 people." With that smile in my spirit and the encouragement of the Lord in my heart, I announced, "Dinner's ready!" Up everyone stood, as they moved into the kitchen to serve themselves. I stood back and watched the pasta instantly replaced as each person filled their plates. After everyone had been served, we were amazed to see virtually the same amount of pasta we started with still in the bowl. Treat everyone like family. Treat everyone like sons and daughters.

Around the Table

Something happens around the dinner table that is no less miraculous than pasta multiplying. When you sit around a table to share food, you are sharing life. In that safe place, you find yourself face to face with people across the table from you. In a moment you have a choice to say nothing or to talk to each other. Talking to each other, being open and honest with each other, grows into knowing each other's heart. When we know each other in the heart of who we really are, the stage is set for God to impart the substance of who He is through us into those who need physical, emotional and spiritual healing.

Caring to know and caring to know what others care about are two different things. I mean the difference between just head knowledge versus head knowledge plus heart knowledge. My granddaughter is six months old and just beginning to what we call *talk*. When the family is sitting around the table eating dinner and talking, we sit Lorelai up in her form-fitted foam seat. Suddenly Lorelai literally starts saying, "Blah, blah, blah, blah, blah, blah, blah, blah...." When she starts talking, everyone stops and pays attention to what she is saying, but she is not saying anything—or is she? I believe she is saying, "I am significant, I am a person, and I am part of this family." As I have listened to what Lorelai has to say, I have been reminded that caring about what she cares about, paying attention to her, looking her in the eyes and giving her my absolute attention is creating something in her that will contribute to her self-esteem and self-worth for years to come.

Full Measure of Trust

Being made to feel like family means when you walk in the door you come in with the full measure of trust. That's the Kingdom starting point, the full measure. In most relationships, you have to earn trust; you have to prove that you belong; you have to show that you are trustworthy. We give the full measure of trust. As a son or a daughter, you are trusted and now you can choose to succeed with that trust or you can make your own choices to break or deteriorate that trust. This is crucial because it helps you to drop performance, to drop any sort of façade, and you can share vulnerably and honestly about the things that are affecting you. When people get treated like sons and daughters, they begin to behave like sons and daughters. You don't have to earn your way in; you don't have to strive to feel valued because you *are* valued. This is addicting because this is what we were wired for.

Needs

Make yourself at home. Are you hungry? Can I make you something to eat? Sit on the couch; relax. Meeting people's physical needs naturally leads to meeting their emotional and spiritual needs. A poverty mindset says, "Go fend for yourself," but when you treat someone like the royalty God intended them to be, you begin to act like the royalty that you are. Ultimately, this is what welcomes someone into a family unit. I am not just going to say, "Make yourself at home" and tell you what is in the fridge. I am going to go beyond warming up what was already made. I am going to find out what you like and want and make that happen. Finding out what a person really wants and is craving and creating that opens the door for what takes place emotionally. I'm going to find out what's going on with you emotionally, what's going on in your day, in your life, where you have come from, how you arrived here, and where you are right now. I am going to spend the time to know what your heart desires and what your heart is hungry for. And I am going to do whatever I can with my life and my resources to cater to that hunger. That's what family does. That's where miracles happen.

FROM HOSPITALITY TO COMMUNITY

Fostering family starts with hospitality but evolves into community. Hosting leads to community which leads to growth. You can continue to show hospitality by continuing to host, but deepening relationships—by creating community, vulnerability, giving, and taking—brings relationships to the next level. I remember a time when we were having a prophetic party at our house and my daughter, Emily, and son-in-law, Victor, were with us for a visit. As we gathered around Victor, Sarah began to prophesy over him by speaking into the things that God had promised him, reinforcing that the Lord had heard and would bring to pass the things Victor had spoken to God about in the secret place. This was a very powerful moment that continued as the atmosphere shifted when Sarah had me stand behind Victor and put my hands on his shoulders to signify this is the papa you have been praying for. Victor has a biological father and an adoptive father, both good men, but Victor was longing for something spiritually that was imparted in that moment that could only happen in that place of family. Since that moment, we have moved into a new place of relationship. I have promised in my heart to be the best papa I can be, and we are committed to grow in the lifelong process of getting to know each other in a way that is only made possible when the Spirit is allowed to bring the growth He establishes through family.

A healthy family understands that sometimes things don't go as expected. I recall a mission trip my daughter took part in that did not turn out the way she expected. They ran out of food and the water filter broke, so they were drinking dirt. One of the students had to be taken to the hospital because of heat stroke, and another got attacked by a bull! Many things about that trip were completely unexpected, but when Emily talks about it now, she talks about how they did it, and how they loved it, and how they had an absolutely great time. Can I remember times in our family that were not so awesome? Have there been times when we hurt each other? Yes, but as long as we are fully aware that family is a journey and that we are committed to the process, then we are open to experience the good that the Lord has for us as we move through the passage of time.

The redemptive power in family is that what once hurt inter-relationally has become a story that we now laugh about. The commitment to each other and our commitment to spending time with the Spirit and seeing things through bring healing. God created family. He is part of our family, and in the context of family by communicating in a healthy way what is going on in our minds, in our hearts, and in our lives, we are transformed by the power of God.

COMMUNICATION

Communicating with each other must come out of love and kindness because the ability to grow together as a family is exponentially greater when you do. Those who don't know how to communicate with love as the driving force lose the ability to see someone for who they are. The discernment needed to see someone's attributes and grab hold of those and pull them out is stunted. People feel and become part of the family because they are seen for who they are, not who they have been or are being right now. The natural, the physical, the emotional, and the spiritual are all connected. Asking God to help you understand and see that connection is an integral step in creating healthy family. Seeing what people need—really well—is a gift that God has for all of us. Some people need a hug while others need to feel at home or to relax or laugh. Seeing those needs and meeting them leads to times when some real in-depth moments in conversation and redeeming prayer occur where we are transformed.

Do you want to move off your present plateau? Do you want to grow? Then find a group of people, a family, who wants that, too. Drop your defenses, become transparent, be open, be honest, be vulnerable, and continue to move from plateau to plateau. In so doing, the ground of your heart will be cultivated and you will be positioned to pour who you have become into others, enabling them to start where you have finished. This is the legacy that rests in the hands of family. This is part of the inheritance you pass to those who will come after you. This is one of the ways you are able to see the hopes and dreams that are in your heart for a happy, healthy family realized.

RELATIONAL HEALTH
—CHAPTER 6—

Since you have purified your souls in obeying the truth through the Spirit in sincere love of the brethren, love one another fervently with a pure heart (1 Pet. 1:22).

Thousands of self-help books on relationships line bookstore shelves. Yet the divorce rate has never been higher, and people persist in finding new ways to avoid face-to-face contact. How much of our interaction occurs through the mediation of our machines? With all the resources we have plus centuries of history to learn from, we still have problems with our relationships. So it seemed right to ask someone who knows how to work with people and has loads of experience helping people at their lowest points to write about relationships. What came out is the answer to why we need so much help: we need the one who is Love to transform us. This chapter gives us an inside glimpse of God's touch on a heart that turns relationships healthy. A healthy relationship with Him sooner or later leads to health in our relationships with others. Read on; wisdom spiced with Southern winsomeness awaits. —P.S.

A Sideways Approach to Healthy Relationships

by Leslie Taylor

ME?

When Pam asked me to write a chapter on healthy relationships, my first response was to be excited and think, *Yes, perfect! I can do that!* My immediate second thought was, *Me? Who am I to write such a chapter?* and I was immediately flooded with thoughts of the relationship "failures" in my life. Pam was reassuring. I immediately felt humbled at the thought of being the author of this chapter.

Unknown to her, the Lord had been talking to me a lot about relationships in the weeks just before this. I fully felt the wind of His pleasure on my accepting this challenge. Quite quickly I also knew that this was not to be just a chapter on the principles of healthy relationships which, as a former marriage and family therapist, I could easily write. Rather, I knew the Lord was directing me to share what He had been showing me about my relationship with myself and with others since moving to Redding. With that, I knew there was no place to be but transparent and vulnerable.

We often hear that we can *teach* what we know, but we can *impart* who we are and what we carry. I freely share from my heart here, in admittedly a bit of a sideways approach to healthy relationships, with the hope that something of worth will be imparted to you as you read about how the Lord showed me unconscious attitudes I had toward people—which served to subtly distance my heart from those I was called to love without reserve. You won't be spoon-fed any conclusions here, and I leave to you and Holy Spirit the task of drawing out what might be applicable to you in your own relationships.

UNFINISHED FORGIVENESS

I was a high-achieving child. Honor roll, honor choir, high school co-valedictorian, *summa cum laude* in college. Very driven and yet never quite reaching my own high standards. It wasn't good enough to get an A+; it had to be the highest A+. I was a perfect textbook example of the "hero child" in family dynamics—even having the classic companions: childhood migraines and an eating disorder in college. And I had almost equally high standards for everyone else. I've always loved people easily—I think more easily than most. But these high standards found expression through a critical spirit. It was a familiar spirit to me, but admittedly these were odd companions.

I actually felt I had gotten a lot of personal victory in this area as a young adult, but the Lord decided it was time to deal a death blow to that critical spirit when I moved to Redding at the age of 50 to attend Bethel School of

Supernatural Ministry. He was kind enough to do it in progressive stages.

The first big work He did in me involved forgiveness. If you had asked me if I carried any unforgiveness in my heart toward anyone at that point in my life, I would have told you no. I had put a lot of hard work into forgiving those who had hurt me. I would have confidently told you that I had forgiven everyone in my life. Of course, I thought forgiveness meant simply speaking forgiveness over them (i.e. "I forgive Johnny").

That all changed one day just weeks into my first year of ministry school. I was calling out to God when all of a sudden, God descended upon me like a warm blanket and lovingly showed me all of the unforgiveness I was holding in my heart toward so many—*including myself*. It was a powerful God encounter. I started sobbing deeply and uncontrollably as so much of the pain deep inside of me came tumbling out.

God showed me in that moment that I had spoken forgiveness over those who had hurt me, but unconsciously I had expected Him to remember what they had done—to still be my champion in the end, to make the wrongs right, and to serve justice. He made me aware of it, and then He gave me the grace to ask Him to completely wipe it from their record like it had never happened in the first place. So much pain flowed out as so much forgiveness was released. I came out of that encounter free of weight I didn't even know I carried!

There was more to come in that process of forgiveness. I remember thinking at the time that at least *now* I had fully forgiven everyone. He would later show me that blessing those who hurt me and really being a champion for good things to happen to them is, what I assumed to be, the final pieces of true forgiveness.

Ah, even now as I type this, He is telling me that there is *another step* to full forgiveness. It is actually *contributing* to the blessing of that person's life—and I am feeling a shift happen in my heart even now in this moment. Selah.

Annoying People

The next big lesson I remember was also early on in that first year of ministry school. There were several young men in my class who seemed to have an excessive need for the spotlight, and they annoyed me. When it was question and answer time, they always had their hand up, going after time with the microphone. When leaders were around, they were right up in front, huddled around them. Annoying.

One day in the middle of one of those critical thoughts, the Lord spoke to me and told me He wanted me to start praying for the one I was grumbling internally about. Ah! I'd been caught! He'd done that to me before. It was familiar territory. I know. I know. I start praying for the ones who annoy me, and then a love for them is kindled in my heart. Yes, and then they become my friends.

That's exactly what happened.

And better yet, because they loved the Lord so much and were pursuing Him, they matured a lot over time. I got to watch the process, and because I had been praying for them, I felt I could even claim a tiny piece of their victory!

Celebrity Kids

God was working hard on my heart. He would always use ways I could relate to. I remember one day I was in my seat, watching students pour in through the doors at the front of the auditorium before class started. He said to me, "How would you treat a classmate who was the son or daughter of someone famous?" I remember envisioning the Bush twins walking through the doors. (George W. Bush was our president at the time.) As He let me think about that for a moment, the children of several celebrities passed through my mind. Then He said, "How do you treat a classmate, knowing they are *My* son or daughter?" I could immediately feel the difference as I watched my "regular" classmates come through the door. Ugh. Caught again!

I was reminded of someone, at church I think, asking us as young kids what would happen if we treated our family members with the same courtesy with which we treated our next door neighbors. That always stuck with me. Now here was God trumping even *that* one. Wow! I would like to say I've never forgotten it, but it would be more honest to say I am constantly reminding myself of what He said. And I hope to get much better at it. How different would our environments be if we treated every single person, not missing one, as the cherished child of the Almighty?

During the second semester of first year, I was looking at someone and courting a small bit of a critical thought about her. The thought was so subtle that I wasn't even fully aware of it. But I became clearly aware of it when all of a sudden I sensed the Lord, quite cheerfully, swing up next to me and sit with me in what appeared to be a witness box where one sits when giving testimony in a courtroom. (As a former police officer, I had sat in those before. It was familiar.)

He pointed to the person I had so quietly criticized and started telling me how much He loved that person and what gifts and strengths He had placed in her. I could feel His pride—the pride of a father. The pride of her Creator. And rather than being overcome with shame, I felt overwhelmed with the beauty He had put into her. I could feel my thoughts toward her shift.

He would do this over and over, day after day. Whenever I had even the slightest, hardly-noticed, negative thought about someone, He would swing up alongside, and there He would be in that box with me, telling me how amazing they were. Every time I could see it, too. His pride and joy fueled my appreciation for them. Soon, I was inviting Him to come and show me the gifts in people I would randomly pick out from the crowd. It got to be a game, and it wasn't long before a real shift in me enabled me to see people more through His eyes than just mine in the natural.

Siding with the Enemy

And I came to learn that the critical side of me that I had always battled wasn't even me. I learned that the enemy talks to us in first person, leading us to believe the thoughts are our own, leading us to come into agreement with them. It finally all made sense! I could never understand how I could be so divided—loving people so much and also being so critical. The more my heart became conformed to God's and how I was created to be, the more I was able to recognize that the voice of the enemy whispering to me was not my own. His tactic was uncovered. Ever since then, whenever I recognize a critical thought entering my head, I just internally respond with, *That's not my thought; get out of here!* and it usually vanishes.

When I am self-critical, it can be more of a challenge. Sometimes I have to just empty my head of any thoughts except one truth, maybe one Scripture that I can focus on and speak over myself until I can take out time to just sit with God for a while and marinate in the goodness of His Presence. And sometimes I need the help of friends, too, who will help me get my thoughts back into alignment with His.

Puppies and Puzzle Pieces

By my second year of ministry school, the Lord had moved in my heart so much that I was now quite partial to my classmates. During first semester, I just soaked in the new-found love I felt for those around me. I could see the beauty in them and the strength in us together.

During the second semester of that second year, God started talking to me about how we were just like a litter of puppies! (We raised Basset Hound puppies when I was a kid.) In fun, He pointed out how we all had the same father (Him) and the same mother (Bethel Church), with each one eventually shipping off to different locations all over the globe. He gave me a vision of us all being different, just like the puppies in a large litter can be. Some of us were big, some were small, some outgoing, some shy, some smart, some not so much. I could picture us in a big pile (which was sometimes true in the natural as well) crawling all over one another just like puppies do. I could imagine that puppies knew nothing of envy or jealousy. They only had fun, living in the moment—and certainly would be proud of their littermates for any recognition or accomplishment.

He also showed me that our class was like a big puzzle—and every piece was important. I enjoy puzzles. There is nothing worse to a puzzle worker than getting down to that very last piece only to find it is missing. When He told me this, I could envision a picture of a big puzzle with a piece missing right out of the middle. The whole picture was affected. He showed me that each piece is vital to the whole. No one could be left behind. I started trying to notice our more hidden classmates, and in my own heart started to value their importance more.

I was feeling an immense amount of loyalty for and protectiveness toward the members of my class. They felt like family, and I was grieved that our time together was about to come to an end. As final goodbyes were being said, a number of people told me I had changed a lot. No one really gave specifics, but I suspected that all the work God had been doing in my heart over the past two years (more than is recorded here) was bearing evidence.

Rescue

Three months after graduation, I was unexpectedly hired by the church to run the Pastor on Call ministry where I had been volunteering. In that ministry, I oversee a team of volunteer lay pastors. Together we minister to people all day long who are struggling with challenges in their lives—often huge and heartbreaking challenges. Sometimes the stories are overwhelming. They can really snowball on you after a while. In the beginning, I found myself quite exhausted and a bit overwhelmed by Friday afternoon each week. A few months into the job, God showed up as rescuer and told me "I am their Savior. Not you. Not Bethel." I so needed that reminder! I put a sign up over my desk with those words, and I look at it and remind myself of its truth every single day.

Trying to help everyone around you will run you ragged pretty quickly. Usually when I get to feeling low after a string of hardship cases, it is because I have forgotten what He told me. I've learned that it is a good truth to remember for any relationship in our lives.

He has taught me to ask Him what my part is and then leave the rest to Him. With our prayers, those we love are in good hands! One time He told me, "You only need two words: *rest* and *trust*." At the time, I felt He was telling me those were the only two words I would *ever* need! Often, when I am really perplexed about what I can do in a challenging relationship, He will tell me my part is just to love, and then rest and trust the outcome to Him. Just hearing Him say that can dissipate all the stress I am feeling and free me to love in a much bigger way. This practice is a very high deterrent to any anxiety or worry we might be carrying for those we love. What a loving, faithful God He is!

Mostly Dirt

As I continued on staff at Bethel, I came to recognize that even in a church environment, not everyone is perfect. (I hope that makes you grin!) At one point, I found myself frustrated at a co-worker and unable to work it out—so I vented my frustration to a couple who have been like spiritual parents to me. They were so loving to me. I think they knew God would reel me in. He did. One day as I continued to seek the Lord for a solution, He said to me, "You know, I let you see the cracks in their foundation because I trust your heart." Then He added, "I trust their heart to your heart." Ah! He has such an amazing way of calling us to higher ground rather than rebuking us for our failures. I love how He does that. (Whenever I feel or hear condemnation, I know it is not Him.)

I immediately felt convicted to give grace and to stand in the gap for what I perceived to be this co-worker's weakness. I felt like God went on to tell me that this person was a part of changing the world, and He had strategically placed me where I was and opened my eyes to see possible weaknesses because He trusted my heart and knew I would cover my co-workers in prayer rather than criticize. I just needed a reminder of who I was.

I should probably add that I have a great amount of esteem for those I work with. I am continually honored to work with incredible men and women who are truly changing the world. One day the Lord said to me, "You know, the only difference between you and them is *risk*." Wow. That was enlightening. It really kind of blew my mind. And it felt like a challenge.

It was a set up. A few months later I was editing a manual for one of our departments and ran across a quote that absolutely stopped my world for a few moments and has wrecked me ever since. It was a quote from our senior associate leader, Kris Vallotton, that went like this: "True prophetic ministry is looking for gold in the midst of the dirt in people's lives." Now having lived here for four years at that time and having gone through the ministry school, I had often heard about calling out the gold in people, a core value here. But what stood out to me when I read this quote was *"in the midst of the dirt."* My mind read it as *"amidst all the dirt."*

Then I heard the Lord say to me, "You expect Christians to be mostly gold with a little bit of dirt. You *especially* expect your leaders to be mostly gold with a little bit of dirt. These leaders know they are imperfect, yet they are still willing to get up on a public stage to be used by Me—dirt and all—knowing it will expose them to gossip, criticism, and judgment, even negative things being written about them. Yet, they are still willing to be used, right now, as they are—and they are changing the world for Me because of it. You are holding yourself back because you are waiting to become mostly gold." It was a profound revelation.

It was at this point that I had a complete shift of perspective. I started expecting everyone to be mostly dirt—myself included! Expectations of near perfection went out the door. Did it really take 55 years for me to see this and accept it?

About this time, I ran across this quote by Henry Wadsworth Longfellow. Perhaps it is a little out of place here, but it comes to mind, and I want to share it with you: "If we could read the secret history of our enemies, we should find in each man's life sorrow and suffering enough to disarm all hostility." I just love that!

THE WHOLE WORLD?

This past year, I found myself praying that everyone in the entire world would be saved and that the whole world would be at peace. As I listened to myself praying this, I felt very childlike. Only a child would pray such a simple, global prayer. I wondered if it was God's will for me to pray for these two things. I knew Second Peter 3:9 tells us that He wants no one to be lost, so I felt pretty aligned with Him in praying for the whole world to be saved. But the Bible tells us there will be wars and rumors of war. I knew He was the Prince of Peace, but for some reason there was a check in my spirit about this, and I wondered if He wanted me to be dedicating time to this prayer—for the entire world to be in peace. I started asking Him if that prayer was His will for me.

A couple of days later, still seeking Him on this, I happened to glance at the clock when it was 1:11 P.M. The numbers 1:11 seemed as though they jumped out at me—almost like they hit me in the face. My first response was to look heavenward and ask, "What was that about?"

I heard, "Zechariah 1:11."

Hmmm. Had my own brain come up with that? Did I imagine that Scripture? "No, it couldn't be," I thought. "I would never think of Zechariah 1:11."

I had no idea what Zechariah 1:11 said, and I was nowhere near a Bible at the time, but later that night I looked it up. It says, *"Then the other riders reported to the angel of the Lord, who was standing among the myrtle trees, 'We have been patrolling the earth, and the whole earth is at peace'"* (NLT). (See Zechariah 1:8-11 for the context.) I had my answer!

As I am reminded about Zechariah 1:11, I pray for peace. Once I get started, I find myself praying with fresh enthusiasm for peace in every home, in every marriage, in every mind and heart and body, in every school, in every board room, in every government office, in every city, in every country, etc. It just flows out of me. I frequently pray quietly from my heart because words can't touch what I want to say to the Lord, but this is a prayer I find myself almost always proclaiming aloud.

I had been praying this for several months when one day, quite out of the blue, the Lord said to me, "You know, world peace begins with you." I knew He wasn't referring to my prayers. He was referring to my choices for peace within myself and in the relationships around me. It made me think of another favorite quote by Mahatma Gandhi: "Be the change you want to see in the world." It really does begin with us—with ourselves and with the person right in front of us.

REWIRING

He continually has more lessons for me, better named *internal adventures*, I think. I have learned that just about the time I think I have "arrived" in some area, God is always faithful to show up and give me a vision for higher ground. I've learned there is always higher ground in the Kingdom.

We had a conference at Bethel this spring. It started with a night service and went for two more days. The first night I had a seat at the back of the auditorium. I stepped out to take an important phone call and left some papers on my chair. I came back to find my chair taken.

The next morning I came in early and this time placed my personal planner on an aisle seat near the back. When I returned to the sanctuary a little bit later, my seat was again taken! *What is wrong with these people?* I thought!

Then during a break, I learned from one of my volunteers that someone had parked in one of our two Pastor on Call (POC) parking spots. A number of my volunteers are beyond 65 years of age, several are in their 80s, and our parking lot gets so full we have to designate two spots for our POC volunteers. They are clearly marked with signs. I was a little stirred up.

And so was my volunteer. I had told him about my seat getting taken twice. He, like me, was incredulous.

That evening in the conference, Pastor Bill Johnson, Bethel's senior leader, was teaching about the political spirit and the religious spirit. He said that people with a religious spirit have an elitist attitude. Right when he said that, God said to me, "You know, you think you are better than *those* people." I knew who He meant. Oh, my! I was stunned. He was right! I was totally convicted. If you had asked me the day before if I had thought I was better than the next guy, I would have told you no. But in that moment, God showed me that I did—at least in this circumstance.

That night and spilling into the next day my volunteer started e-mailing me about our experiences that day. He was really disturbed by the sense of entitlement he felt he was seeing. In his e-mailing, he asked me what we could do about this entitlement problem. I responded that we should sow honor and humility. He wanted to know what I meant, and I explained that just as Pastor Bill had taught us to sow generosity where there was a poverty mindset, we could shift the atmosphere where there is entitlement by showing honor and humility.

I confessed to him what the Lord had shown me the previous evening when Pastor Bill spoke. My volunteer was as convicted as I was; we had been so indignant. Now we were both humbled at our own pride.

The Lord showed me that when people have weaknesses or make poor decisions that I can relate to and therefore understand, I am able to show a great amount of grace. It is when people make poor choices that I cannot relate to in any way that I sometimes allow a superior attitude to creep into my heart. Ugh! He showed me another area of my life where that attitude had crept in. He was conforming my heart to His and, at the same time, better suiting me for my destiny and the desires of my heart.

GOD'S QUESTION

A few days after that conference, I was in our early morning staff prayer time. The moment I entered the room and found a place on the floor to sit, I saw again that puzzle with the piece missing out of the middle. Though I have thought of it from time to time, it had been three years since He showed it to me. This time I felt He was showing me that I was that piece in the middle, and before He could place me there, He had one question to ask me: "Are you willing to link arms with whomever I put beside you?"

I immediately thought of difficult people in my life. I felt a switch occur in my heart again, and I replied, "Yes, Lord, I am."

It is so important in relationships that we focus on the good in others and not the bad. That we focus on what God is doing in their lives and not what we haven't yet seen answered, because *whatever we focus on grows*. It is so true what Pastor Bill says, "We cannot afford to have a thought in our head that isn't in His." We must pull our thoughts into alignment with His (see 2 Cor. 10:5) to love as He does. The Word tells us:

> *Finally, brethren, whatever things are true, whatever things are noble, whatever things are just, whatever things are pure, whatever things are lovely, whatever things are of good report, if there is any virtue and if there is anything praiseworthy—meditate on these things* (Philippians 4:8).

I think this might be one of the most important verses in the Bible! And this principle is just as true for our thoughts about ourselves as it is for others.

EXTREME LOVE

It is so important to Jesus that we love one another. He listed it as a summation of the Law (see Luke 10:25-28) and gave it as a new command shortly before His death. He said that we should love each other *just as He has loved us*, and from this the world would know that we are His followers (see John 13:34-35). His heart for us is to have the same extreme love He and our Father share for one another.

Obviously, the Lord is not done with me yet, but it excites me to watch my response to fully love become more *naturally* me. I hope my story ignites transformation in your own relationships, wherever it might be needed, because I truly believe that the more we walk in extreme love for one another, the more we will see Heaven coming to earth and His glory manifesting among us.

CREATIVE HEALTH

—CHAPTER 7—

Then the Lord spoke to Moses, saying: See, I have called by name Bezalel the son of Uri, the son of Hur, of the tribe of Judah. And I have filled him with the Spirit of God, in wisdom, in understanding, in knowledge, and in all manner of workmanship, to design artistic works, to work in gold, in silver, in bronze, in cutting jewels for setting, in carving wood, and to work in all manner of workmanship (Ex. 31:1-5).

Reading Exodus 31 recently, I noticed that the same chapter that revealed the first person in the Bible ever to be called "anointed"—Bezalel, an artisan—also included God's heart about the Sabbath. The artisans were set aside (made holy) to create the set apart things for the tabernacle, also holy. And God mentioned the setting apart of that holy day for His holy, set apart people to rest. There is so much to ponder in this chapter, but what strikes me is the relationship between creativity and rest. When we enter into rest with the Lord—both physically as in having a Sabbath, and spiritually, as in the rest of Hebrews 4—our creativity is allowed to bubble to the surface.

Engaging our creative life is part of the health of the abundant life in the Lord. "Creative" doesn't necessarily mean artistic in the sense of the fine arts, but the arts are certainly a part of it. Expressing our creativity in any way is so therapeutic that universities issue degrees in music therapy, art therapy, and dance therapy. Neurologist Dr. Oliver Sacks has shown that Alzheimer's patients do not lose their ability to play music, and that playing music activates their brains. In April 2012, Good Morning America aired a segment entitled, "Alzheimer's Disease: Music Brings Patients 'Back to Life.'"[1]

Life! This chapter is written by one who has seen many people renewed (and even healed) as they engaged in their creative side.—P.S.

Our Creative God

by Theresa Dedmon

As I sit looking out at my panoramic view of a beautiful sunset, I am reminded of how God loves to create beauty for me and for all His children and how that beauty continues to unfold with every second we are alive. We discover His many creative languages through nature, people, places, and key events when He carves our name with His on the tree trunk of our lives. It's simple. We are loved. This truth is not stagnant, but is masterfully woven with sound, movement, color, texture, and form, designed to reflect the relational aspects of what brings joy and life.

I couldn't imagine a life without God's creativity, reflecting the diversity and immensity of what love looks like through the works of the Creator of the universe. As we peek through the dramas in Scripture, we become engrossed in the stories of His interventions and demonstrations of love toward us. Just take a moment and explore God's diversity and beauty in nature and the world. His creativity has a humorous side; for instance, just think about the way He created the bizarre-looking animals, reptiles, and insects. He really has a flair for detail and beauty. Creativity is not stagnant but continues to unfold with every budding flower and seasonal transition. He has created different experiences for us through taste, smell, sight, sound, and touch. His creativity is endless, intriguing, and mysterious. Creativity is healing, and when we look at His handiwork, we get in touch with who He is and how we are made.

All of Us Are Creative!

If we are *created* in God's image (see Gen. 1:27), we have the ability to create, to bring life and beauty all around us. God has always desired man to partner with Him in creativity. Man's first task was to name the animals, declaring their nature and DNA (see Gen. 2:19). After that, God created woman, and immediately man named her and prophesied her destiny because he understood from naming the animals previously what his role would be as a creative force for good. He partnered with the Creator of the universe, shaping her potential by calling out her role in life. Our role as His children is to restore man's identity back to the Father and to be reconcilers. The way we do this should be as varied as the ways we are designed and reflect His nature through us. This is why the Gospels share four very different accounts of the life of Jesus. Each apostle had a certain passion, desire, and creative make-up that came out as he wrote and shaped his narrative from his perspective.

We partner with what the Father is saying by bringing Heaven to earth through what we create with our words, body, and heart. If we are to tap into this truth, we need to rediscover our role in being creative, prophetic sons and daughters, who are all different in the way that we display the Father's heart. Without His presence, our unique creative call is flat and powerless. God in any equation changes the outcome. Let's look at how others have tapped into their relationship with the Father, releasing the Holy Spirit's presence through creativity.

I was sharing with my creativity students in our school of ministry at Bethel about the miracles that can be released through creativity. One of my first-year students began to partner her creativity with a family need. She wanted to touch her sister, who wasn't walking with God, when she went home for Christmas that year. So she decided to paint a breakthrough painting, using different colors and shapes to create an opening for her sister to encounter God's love for her. That Christmas, she gave the painting to her sister, who hung it up in her living room. A couple of days later, her sister's three-year-old woke up crying as he did every night. Instead of having him stay in his room, she decided to try to get him to settle down in the living room, where the painting was hanging. As she went in there, astonishingly, he stopped crying. Her husband woke up, and as he came into the living room, he fell down under the presence of God, unable to move for hours. In the morning, her sister received a text about the significance of the painting she had given and how they wanted God in their lives!

One time when I was teaching a workshop on healing through creativity, a man who had carpal tunnel syndrome and couldn't play the piano anymore began to realize how God's goodness could transform his situation. After I shared testimonies about people being healed during the workshop, he creatively began to draw his own hands on a piece of paper in blue, symbolizing the revelation he had just received from the testimonies I had just shared, and then he added red to his hands, signifying the blood of Jesus. He then tested out his hands to see if they were painful—and he was completely healed!

Are You Creative?

God's power works through His children creatively to bring healing to the body, soul, and spirit. When, by partnership with the Holy Spirit, we create something that no one else can, we can bring transformation through a simple song, an innovative business strategy, or creative solutions to a problem. If we create in His presence, we can also find the healing that we need and find restoration in our personal lives. But for many of us, this is a foreign concept. Bill Johnson, in his book *Hosting the Presence,* shares insights into how our lack of understanding about creativity limits the Body of Christ:

> One of the great mysteries in life is to see the descendants of the Creator show so little creativity in how we do church and life in general. I don't think that lack comes from people who like to be bored or who like to control things to death. It usually comes from a misunderstanding of who He is and what He is like. People often fear being wrong so much that they fail to try something new, thinking they will displease God. If more people would relax in His goodness, we'd probably give a more accurate expression of the God who is never boring. He is still creative. And it's in our nature to be the same.[2]

We find out who we are and what we are born to do through enjoying His presence. We are the message, shaping and influencing culture to reflect His goodness upon the earth. Our role in history is to release the manifest presence of God through our creative nature to bring revival. In this place, we move from a passive and dormant life to one of color, brilliance, ideas, and solutions. God wants us to live with miracles as our daily diet, and creativity holds keys to breaking this realm of miracles open in our lives.

In the Old Testament, we have an account about how Moses partnered with creativity to heal the Israelites. In Numbers 21:4-9, we find that the Israelites were being bitten by snakes, causing death. They came to Moses and repented for speaking against leadership. God then directed Moses to "create" a bronze serpent, which if the people *looked at* would bring life and not death. In other words, God partnered with Moses' creativity to supernaturally bring healing to others— by looking at what He had made. Also, I am reminded about how the demon would leave King Saul when David played the harp. God's design is for the power of His presence to actually dispel darkness as we partner with His Holy Spirit through creative expressions. In other words, David released God's presence not through just praying or preaching, but through bringing God's presence *as* he played. We don't know what we carry. God is awakening so many creative strategies to His people for wholeness and healing. Just ask the Holy Spirit what you carry and what to release in situations that seem hopeless. You carry the DNA of Heaven and will see miracles of healing.

CREATIVITY IN DIVINE PARTNERSHIP RELEASES MIRACLES

One of the places at Bethel Church where many people receive healing is in our Healing Rooms. We have people and children trained in art, dance, and music who create an "Encounter Room," where people who are sick can come and encounter God.

One Saturday, a person with terminal brain cancer came into the Healing Rooms. She was asked to stare at a painting that had the word "hope" written on it. As she stared at the painting, the tumor oozed out of her ear, and she was healed miraculously! This painting was then brought into one of Bethel's services and a man who was diagnosed with bipolar disorder and depression heard the testimony and began to look at it. As he did, he also was instantaneously healed as well! He no longer needed medication and now is an artist himself, releasing supernatural power through what he creates.

On a ministry trip, one of my team was sharing about these testimonies, and a woman who was profoundly deaf in one ear felt liquid coming out of her ear. She took out her hearing aide, tested out her hearing, and was completely healed! God supernaturally anoints what we create in His presence to release physical, mental, and spiritual healing. The testimonies of these miracles can release healing even without anyone praying because faith and God's creative power are always available.

Dance can also be a way that people are healed. Parents who were desperate for a miracle for their daughter who had leukemia gave one of our dancers, Saara Taina, a key chain, which had her daughter's picture on it, as their daughter was too sick to come for prayer. As Saara danced in the Healing Rooms, power was released to their daughter. They took her to the doctor the following week, and there was no more cancer! We are to dance over the injustices in this world. Cancer has to die when exposed to the healing power of God!

I head up a ministry called "Impart Arts in Healing" that is now a part of a program in one of our local hospitals. We are able to minister to people body, soul, and spirit through dance, art, and music. A man in the hospital in ICU was brain dead, and his parents were thinking of taking him off life support. One of our team went in and began to sing and play the guitar, releasing healing to his body and hope to his parents. All of a sudden, he began to move his legs! A week later he was moved to another room, where our prophetic art cards from our team hung around his bed. He now is out of the hospital, and his parents have asked us to continue to visit him. Creativity through the arts has brought healing and transformation to the hopeless, where they receive life in the midst of tragedy.

I have been equipping others around the world in creativity and have found that if we ask Holy Spirit what He is doing and partner with His presence, our creativity carries miraculous power for healing. This happens through dance, art, music, singing, and any other creative act or form God shows a person. We carry an anointing that is transferrable, just like in Acts 19:11, where Paul's handkerchiefs healed people as they touched them. You may ask, how is this possible or why would God do this? I would like to propose to you that He has *always* wanted to partner our creativity with His presence, but we have never explored the many ways that God touches and brings life to His people. But that is changing.

SANCTIFIED IMAGINATION

Proverbs 27:3 says that *as a man thinks in his heart, so is he.* In other words, your imagination about yourself and your situation is creatively manifesting life or death for your body, soul, and spirit. We all need to pay attention to what we believe. Most people have allowed what others think of them or what society thinks to determine who they are. This can lead to all different kinds of problems—body, soul, and spirit. If we create boxes in our imaginations about who we are and live inside of them, the true self that God created will never be seen. What if Job had allowed the thoughts of his friends and wife to take control of his imagination and future? They weren't living from Heaven's reality, but from the enemy's assault. What happens when we allow others who don't have a sanctified imagination to determine who we are? This will lead to all different kinds of problems because we were never meant to live in anyone else's shadow or image, as we were created in our mother's womb to reflect God's image in our unique make-up.

A LITTLE CHILD SHALL LEAD

At what age does a person determine to play it safe and stop being herself? When this happens, creativity and originality are lost. Let's take a look at children to determine God's intent. You don't have to tell children to play or to create; just go to any preschool and watch them! They automatically begin to use their imagination to create through dance, art, writing, and play. They have no fear about sharing what they have done because they know it's good. Only as they grow up do they fear others seeing them play, create, dance, write, paint, and use their imagination to think outside the box of the norms of the day.

"I Don't 'Feel' Creative"

You may think, "Well, I'm not creative." Creativity is not something some are born with and others are not. Every seed-bearing plant reproduces after its own kind. In the same way, we are made like our heavenly Father, and are therefore creative by nature. The problem arises because we have not *believed* creativity is valuable or given to every person. Bill Johnson comments on this misunderstanding that many have: "Creativity is the touch of the Creator on every part of life. It's the need of the accountant and the lawyer as much as it is for the musician and actor. It is to be expected when you're the son or daughter of the Creator, Himself."[3] God has designed every person with different facets that reflect Him. He is a God of detail; just look at the elaborate details for Noah building the ark, Moses constructing the Ark of the Covenant, and Solomon ingeniously crafting the temple. Take a look at how Jesus taught through parables and healed people through different ways. Our creativity and encounters with God are all different because He comes to us through who we *are,* not generically. He is a God who is personal, and this is how He wants us to be.

Blocks to Supernatural Creativity

When the creative juices inside of us are suppressed or hidden, our body, soul, and spirit can be negatively affected. We were born to create like our heavenly Father, and when we don't open up to this creativity, we become stuck. Everyone alive has a creative potential and playful side that needs to be valued and explored. One of my greatest privileges in life is helping people gain freedom from fears and insecurities that keep them from exploring their ability to create. A child will create things freely without fearing making a mistake or displeasing others. On the other hand, if you asked adults to sing, write, or draw a picture for someone, many would have knots in their stomach, unable to complete simple tasks. It's time that we stop feeling anxiety or fear when we express ourselves creatively. God is delighted when His children are free to express themselves without fear of failure or measuring up.

In Scripture, God never wanted us to be afraid to express what's on the inside or to wonder if it is valuable. When we read Psalm 139, we find that we are fearfully and wonderfully made. God doesn't make junk, and He doesn't feel that you create junk. Neither should you!

Our educational system, as well as society, has developed a culture where people are afraid to really be who they are. They are afraid of being different, not measuring up, or failing to meet the standard. This structure closes down creativity and our unique nature. So many people have to hide who they really are behind trying to look a certain way to fit in, plastic smiles, or trying to be like those they esteem. When you try to be something you're not, you feel disconnected inside, which manifests in sickness or appearing phony. This then comes out in physical problems, disorders like anorexia, obesity, depression, or self-hatred. This cycle can make us feel powerless, devalued, or ugly. If we can't embrace who we truly are, then we can't find out the destiny that has been waiting for us. There is no one like you! Be proud that you carry the marks of the Creator God in you, body, soul, and spirit, and live free from conforming to any standard that robs you of being who God created you to be.

So right now, as you read this chapter, I want you to let go of all the fears and insecurities that you have believed about how God has designed you to be. Embrace the realization that you *are* creative and unique. Let your *real* self out. Go ahead, paint a picture, sing a song, find a creative solution to business, or go after your dreams. Believe that you were born for a purpose and a destiny as Jeremiah 29:11 points out, and that you display a unique facet of God that no one else can. In this place of security, knowing you are made in your Father's image, the greatest potential will be realized. So let go of fear and hold on to His promises over your life and find out who you are designed to be.

DOUBTING THE SUPERNATURAL POWER OF GOD

Another issue that stops people from releasing healing through their creativity is lack of experience in the supernatural ways of God. Many people have never seen how creativity and the supernatural are linked together. Again, if we are made in His image, we *are* creative, and if we have the Holy Spirit's power, signs and wonders will follow (see Mark 16:17). Therefore, we must go after the greater works God promised us, and they will not be found by following a formula, but by us learning to partner with the Holy Spirit in every situation. We have not because we ask not. So go after supernatural creativity, and ask the Holy Spirit for something that would break into the life of someone you know or will meet. Make a card, sing a song, release a dance, ask for a creative strategy, or write a piece that will release healing and life. As you move out into your supernatural creative destiny, life will flow through you, and your wellbeing will increase.

Presence Versus Performance

If we are constantly feeling inferior, then we will strive to be accepted. Just like a vine cannot produce fruit by straining, we cannot produce fruit by trying to be good enough. As we let go and create and learn to be significant through being in His presence, then we can enjoy our creative nature and who we were born to be without giving in to what others think. God wants us to learn to see ourselves as God sees us and to accept ourselves because He loves us the way we are. End of story, period.

God Values All of You

I remember when I was growing up I wanted to be a nun and teacher. My husband, Kevin, is glad that I never became a nun—but my call to know and serve God came to me at an early age. I also came from a highly creative family. When I graduated from high school, I could have received an art scholarship, but declined so that I could pursue ministry. I didn't think that art was valuable to God because I never saw this modeled in church. But, now I see how creativity can preach—just as much as a sermon. Whatever passions and interests we have are valuable to God because they make us happy and fulfilled. If it matters to us, it matters to God. These passions will be the places where we can experience the most breakthrough in releasing healing. I am truly fulfilled when all of me has a voice for the Father and can be activated in the Kingdom. I no longer doubt if who I am is relevant because every part of my life reflects Him and has supernatural power to heal and prophesy.

BODY OF CHRIST COMES ALIVE!

Wherever I go, I have stacks of testimonies from people thanking me for giving them permission to create and be released from the critical words of the past that have made them doubt their creativity and value. It's so rewarding to see people's faces come alive as they're valued for what they alone can create and are equipped to see others healed or encouraged through partnership with the Holy Spirit. I was speaking at a church in Hawaii, where we equipped the church to go out into the community, releasing supernatural creativity. We saw so many people get healed and set free! The pastor's wife was very new to exploring her partnership with creativity but went ahead and drew a picture of a house with a red roof when we were at the park. She felt it was for family restoration. She finally had the courage to give away her piece of art to a man standing by the playground. As she approached, she hesitantly showed him her picture and shared the word about restoration. She then asked him if this meant anything to him. His eyes got as big as saucers as he explained to her that he had come to the park to meet his estranged wife to see if they could be reconciled! When the wife showed up, he explained the picture to her. They were reconciled and brought back together through a simple picture bringing healing and confirmation to a man who didn't know that God was there. This is the power of supernatural creativity that you and I can access.

Creativity Keeps us Whole and Thriving

On a ministry trip to North Dakota, I went to a premier care facility for the aged to bring a culture of celebration through creativity to the elderly. I had the privilege of meeting a 102-year-old woman who had just graduated from college two years before. She gave me her book and was so excited when one member of my team danced a healing dance to impart life for her. She was animated, fully alive, and still productive. The smile on her face spoke louder than words. Her desire to learn and to create was still going strong. She still had something to say and give to the world.

I believe that the apostle Paul talks about how we need to live in a constant state of learning and going after the more just like this centenarian woman: *"Not that I have already obtained all this, or have already been made perfect, but I press on to take hold of that for which Christ Jesus took hold of me"* (Phil. 3:12 NIV).

Our aim is not to struggle to gain significance to feel better about who we are. Rather, we are to ask God to use who we are in our creative nature to understand who He is and what He did in setting us free. Therefore, the supernatural power is tied to our identity in Christ and not to an ability or an event. We are designed to be His ambassadors, so we need to know what He is about and reflect His nature. Using our creativity for His glory and reflecting His nature will be our highest fulfillment.

GAINING ACCESS

Here are some tools to help you begin the journey toward healing through creativity.

- Embrace your unique make-up and the way that God created you.

- Become like a child and enjoy His presence as you create, breaking off fear and performance.

- Partner with the Holy Spirit and create things that bring healing to you or others. Ask the Father to show you His heart and how to be activated.

- Explore your passions and how you are designed to enjoy life and God's presence.

- Ask God to partner your unique creative design with His supernatural power for healing and transformation to those you meet both in the church and in the marketplace.

As revival comes, healing begins to break out, and people begin to be free to experience God through dance, art, writing, and laughing, and they enter into their role as a child of God—free to be different and to play. This sets their sanctified imagination free and brings them into a relationship with God not as a tyrant, but as a loving Father who enjoys His children's creativity and individuality. If we come to Jesus, we must come to Him as a child, and in this place we must see how much He enjoys how we are made. God wants us to re-create by resting in His presence and by allowing ourselves to enjoy just being with Him.

ENDNOTES

1. Katie Moisse, "Alzheimer's Disease: Music Brings Patients 'Back to Life'" ABC News, April 12, 2012, accessed October 09, 2012, http://abcnews.go.com/ Health/AlzheimersCommunity/alzheimers-disease-music-brings-patients-back-life/story?id=16117602.

2. Bill Johnson and Heidi Baker, *Hosting the Presence: Unveiling Heaven's Agenda* (Shippensburg, PA: Destiny Image Publishers, 2012).

3. Ibid., 176.

FINANCIAL HEALTH
—CHAPTER 8—

Whoever can be trusted with very little can also be trusted with much... (Luke 16:10 NIV).

Sooner or later, getting really healthy will affect our wealth. The result could be as simple as our finally learning to live within our means and enjoying a quiet and peaceable life. Or it could mean that we have prospered and, faithful, have been entrusted with "much" to become financers of great Kingdom enterprises. Either way, God cares about our financial lives. Jesus spoke a lot about money. Money can be a great test of our character and our spiritual health. Jesus came to redeem us from the curse of the law. And in His redemption is also a redeemed relationship to money. To write this chapter, I chose one who I knew not only himself lives in a healthy relationship to money but has been able also to help many others to find the balance in their financial lives. In fact, his ministry at Bethel has contributed to Bethel's smooth transition from local church to church, school and movement while retaining financial integrity. Along with the other leaders on the senior team, he has made sound and healthy financial choices that keep us safe. Beyond the wisdom he imparts is an anointing from the Lord to set people free, open their eyes, and help them realize dreams. King Solomon's life of peace and blessing is an example of what it looks like when God gets to bless a person and a people as much as He would like to. We do well to ponder Solomon's life and to find out what God would like to do for us and through us for the sake of others. Read this chapter with anticipation of what the Lord can do for you in the realm of finances. —P.S.

Healing Our Finances

by Stephen K. De Silva

Jesus came down...and those who were troubled with unclean spirits were being cured. And all the people were trying to touch Him, for power was coming from Him and healing them all (Luke 6:17-19 NASB).

Jesus cured the sick and troubled. Today, He still moves within reach, releasing the power to heal on every willing soul. He is salvation, Himself, bringing so complete a healing that the demonized become whole. In Luke 8:35, the account of a demoniac man's complete and full recovery shocked those who knew him. Here was the man, healed in his body (fully clothed), delivered in his soul (being in his right mind), and saved in his spirit (seated resting at Jesus' feet). How Christ cures disease in every form is profound. And this healing power even comes to one's finances—perhaps especially to one's finances.

I make this assertion because money is itself a spiritual power, exaggerating whatever lies hidden in a person's heart. We all have heard stories of power handled poorly. Any spiritual powers can be handled honorably or foolishly; regardless, power will always exaggerate what we *believe* from our hearts.

Powers are like fertilizer, belief like seed. Powers make seeds thrive and bear fruit after their kind. Some seed is good, yielding blessings and benefits; let's name this good seed *truth*. Some seed is bad, and yields sorrow, loss, and destructive cycles; let's name that bad seed *lies*.

Receiving a healing in your finances means allowing God to displace every lie that you harbor in your heart. By harbor, I mean *believe*. And what we believe dictates our actions; this is the law of roots. We can resist this law for a time, but only with great effort. When you believe lies about money, the lie performs like a seed with the potential to bear painful and sinful fruit in your life. Replace the lies with truth, however, and you have a different harvest. Truth under the influence of money causes that truth to flourish. Another way to say this is that money exaggerates the truth hidden in your heart. And truth exaggerated means blessing and benefits exaggerated, poured out, and aimed at the assignments of Christ. This, then, is the purpose of money: to accomplish the purposes of Christ. Every place in your life where Christ is not well-represented through your money reveals a place needing financial healing. So the key to healing in your finances comes down to recognizing financial lies—call it *financial disease*—that you harbor in your heart. Let's look at some examples of financial disease.

Provision

One common evidence of financial disease is found in the area of your thoughts. When it comes to money, what do you think about? What goes through your grey matter when you see an article in the news about the depressed economy? Or when someone asks for money, what thoughts go through your mind? If you wander toward worry, then you may have found the fingerprint of a struggle with provision.

God is our source, but we can become focused on our need when we believe a lie about provision. This core belief may feel true, but the lie that we are on our own cannot help but deliver worry and toil. For some, the continual grappling with fear over provision can be tormenting. If you have such a condition, let's deal with this now. Repeat this prayer with me:

Father God, what is the lie I am believing about provision?

Allow yourself a moment to listen or feel His reply. The answer usually comes so quickly it catches you by surprise. If you have trouble hearing from Father God, it is usual to conclude that you are broken. Know that this, too, is a lie; it is far more likely that you are over-working the exercise. If you feel driven by desperation and fear, understand these are clear symptoms of a lie believed. Christ is a shepherd; sheep are led, not driven. You are not broken; God doesn't make broken things. However, you may have experienced a lifetime of lies and attacks and may suffer from a thorough *denting*. So let's go one step further for those who are unpracticed in hearing well. Pray this aloud:

Father God, you are the Maker; there is none beside you. I am your creation. And whether I have been close or far, you remain my Maker. I know you hear my prayers, Father. Now cause my heart to heal. Displace the lie that I cannot hear with the truth. What is the truth, Father God?

Listen for an affirming word from God. Recognize the first thing you hear, see, or sense that sounds like love speaking.

Father, I heard you say _____ [fill in what you believe He said or showed you]. *And every part that agrees with perfect love, I ask you to fold it deeply into my soul. Create a clean heart and right spirit in me, Father, that I would hear and believe your provision and walk in supernatural peace. In Jesus' name I ask. Amen.*

Write down what you heard, and place it somewhere you will regularly see it. Since we become what our eyes behold, take care what you set before you. Be sure to feed on truth and not lies.

KINGDOM ECONOMY

Christians rarely speak in terms of healing from financial disease, but let's press on and bravely look at some other symptoms. Consider your last five to ten years: what do you see? Are you growing stronger financially? Are you building wealth to pass on to your children's children—two generations? Are your investments growing, or have they slipped under corrosive economic times? Has your debt grown or shrunk? To excuse eroding wealth because of trends in local or national economics is tempting, but be careful. Believers are not immune to regional economics, but we also participate in a heavenly economy that knows no limits. We are not victims! The Kingdom economy works; it looks like favor. It's the kind of favor that left the Queen of Sheba "breathless" (see 2 Chron. 9:4 NASB).

Under the Kingdom economy, a believer's home should enjoy a better favor. God is a rewarder (see Heb. 11:6), and His reward will work to evangelize the world (see Mal. 3:12). I call this an evangelism of jealousy, where the unbelieving nations recognize we are blessed. Take the housing bubble, for example. Believers and unbelievers alike were purchasing homes in the early 2000s. Both had opportunity to purchase beyond their financial capacity because that was the agreed-upon procedure from lenders of the day. Acting as a massive stimulant for the national economy, the government and regulators both agreed and encouraged what is now decried as predatory lending practices. But it was always the consumers who were deciding to purchase the houses and who signed the contracts promising to repay the huge mortgages.

I had my turn in early 2000. I felt God had said to sell our first home and upgrade to something larger for our young family of four. After all the science, we qualified for a much larger loan than we expected and were dizzy with the possibilities. But Dawna and I had a modest list of needs and fewer wants. Those needs and wants were shaped by our purpose in life, a belief in a destiny much greater than ourselves. We saw ourselves becoming a Joseph someday, becoming a couple who would silo wealth for the sake of others (see Gen. 39:4). Our giving goals dictated our living goals, and this was the "top down" approach we felt God would bless. So, we chose a house that was modest by our pre-approval standards. Five years later, our capacity to borrow was even higher and newer, bigger houses tested our resolve. But our purpose dictated a different set of priorities, so we kept to our simple lifestyle. Debt was declining in our lives, assets were growing, and we were inconspicuously prospering along with the rest of the US economy. Our favor was masked until the 2008 housing bubble burst.

Everyone's highly inflated home values fell over the next four years. My $145,000 home had doubled to $350,000 at its peak, but when the bubble popped, I watched the value shrink down, down, down. As of this writing, we still live in that house (which proves the miracle). I would estimate its value at under $200,000. But the Kingdom economy had worked in my home. During the bubble mania, we never borrowed more than we could pay, and what we did borrow was tempered by our priorities rather than status and luxury. Our net worth in the home took a bloody fall, but never fell below the mortgage. Our faithful and quiet life choices, combined with God's mercy at providing our incomes, have placed us in a position to give financial strength during tough economic times. When others had need, we were able to give intentionally and strategically as the Holy Spirit directed.

That testimony is not a boast, but a prophetic declaration (see Rev. 19:10) that you and I are meant to behave as Joseph in Pharaoh's court—even in the years of plenty (see Gen. 41:48). For sure, people have had a terrible time passing through this recession, and there will likely be more trouble ahead. But it will pass! And when it passes, it will be our honor and duty to live with Christ's priorities and not our own. It will be our chance at experiencing the Kingdom economy in our very homes.

If you have suffered under the pain of loss during this recent recession, I have great news for you. The worst is behind you. Continue to hope. Shake off discouragement and despair. God is a deliverer, and you are in His hands! When we are pressed and needing rescue, there is never a question of *if* but *when* God will come through. God always does, and your situation will not be your demise. Lies lodged in your heart that shout that you will be overlooked or forgotten will only produce fear and reckless behavior. Breathe! Watch and pray, expecting your breakthrough. When it comes, fly your gratitude like a banner and renew your priorities for Kingdom living.

If you are in financial strength now, realize the real test still stands before you. Learn how to carry your blessings under the direction of the Holy Spirit. It may be harder than you think. Most people do well spiritually when they are tight, relying on their need to drive them to prayer. But this model depends upon trouble to provoke spiritual sensitivity. Imagine living in a way where strength and success drive you to prayer instead of trouble. It would create a sensitivity driven by blessing. What a different paradigm. If you want a spiritual life that is led by blessing, repeat this prayer with me:

> *Father God, you are the giver of all good gifts. And I am your grateful steward. I am a manager of your secrets* (1 Cor. 4:1). *Show me how to sow and save. Make me into a Joseph, doing good in this world, in order to preserve many lives* (Gen. 50:20). *In Jesus' name I ask. Amen.*

Listen for direction, and write down every instruction you hear, sense, or see. Learn to practice this skill, as Hebrews 5 commands.

Playing the Hero

Every good story contains a victim, a villain, and a hero. Most of us spend our lives jumping between the three roles, driven by our circumstances and situations rather than our purpose. How would your life change if you played the hero, affecting your circumstances rather than being led by them? How would that change affect your decisions with money?

Practical financial skills are easy to find. There are many excellent authors and teachers who answer questions and offer advice on money. I will finish this chapter with my own rendition of some practical steps for playing the hero (being intentional) with your finances. But remember, mastering money, riches, and wealth is an inside job. The heart matters more than actions because behaviors will only change permanently when we deal with what we believe about money and ourselves. We always act out of what we believe. So let's move ahead under a presumption that truth about money is rooted in your heart. Let's begin to discuss how health in your finances looks at a practical level.

80/10/10

There are lots of prescriptions about money. We can declare it in, demand it in, claim it in—but these methods all betray an underlying spirit of entitlement. We are not entitled to money; we are merely privileged to steward. Beware of the financial "laws of attraction." Although I agree in concept, it is wrongly applied to the subject of money. The command of money has one foot in biblical truth, the other in the error of ancient Babel. We are to be purpose-driven, and once money becomes the lead motive, you have sounded the summons for the spirit of Mammon. Instead, attracting money should "ensue" and not be pursued. Like Victor Frankl said, you don't pursue success or happiness; those things must *ensue* and become the result or product of serving something or Someone greater than yourself. I apply the idea in this way: financial health should follow your life like a shadow racing behind you, following as you "happen." I don't pursue financial health; I walk in faithfulness and watch it ensue.

Financial decisions in my house are directed by our giving priorities. It has long been that way and works very simply. Dawna and I use a simple budgeting method of only three categories: Living, Giving, and Saving. Every dollar spent fits into one of those three categories.

Living is the group that carries every dollar of spending in your life, including debt service. Your auto and home costs are included here, along with your personal care and your pets. Everything to do with your life goes under this broad title. The second category is *Giving*, meaning your tithes and offerings. For my household, we settle on 10 percent tithe as a minimum for our generosity. This is from the biblical reference to the tithe (which literally means "tenth"). My personal giving goal is 25 percent, although I'll confess I began at zero until I learned better, and I have yet to reach that goal. I love to give as a form of worship. When we withhold the tithe, the devourer of Malachi 3:10-12 comes to take it. When we do tithe, God promises to rebuke the devourer on our behalf. Either way, it appears the tithe will be given whether we offer it or not. I recommend a generous lifestyle of tithing plus additional offerings.

If I give 10 percent as a minimum, I am forced to live on the remaining 90 percent. But wait, there's one more category: *Saving*. A key behavior of financial healing is mounting saving. I suggest a savings goal of matching your savings with whatever percentage you give. In my example, you would give a 10 percent tithe as a minimum and match that percentage with a savings of 10 percent, leaving a budget of 80 percent of total spending on all living costs. Hence the formula: 80/10/10. Looking years ahead, I suggest aiming at growing your giving and saving goals as you are able. Below is a table showing an initial target and two future models as examples.

CATEGORY	PERCENTAGE OF ALL SPENDING	10-YEAR GOAL (suggestion)	20-YEAR GOAL (suggestion)
LIVING	80%	70%	60%
GIVING	10%	15%	20%
SAVING	10%	15%	20%

This is a lofty goal for Americans who continue to live at or beyond their incomes. Based on census studies, most of us look like this: 98/2/0. There have been seasons when the average American model twists to 101/0/-1. That means an average person's living costs exceed what he earns, he gives nothing to charities, and he experiences a negative savings rate (consumer debt). This model is understandable for temporary seasons like college years or temporary unemployment, but it cannot be a long-term strategy. Sadly, it is exactly this last model that has brought the average US citizen to a nationwide cliff walk. Our solution will be found in personal wealth, not through artificial stimulation to the economy through debt-based spending. It will be a long road, but Americans will learn to live within our means. The church should lead this quiet economic revolution. We can no longer live beyond our means as a nation and presume no day of reckoning. I find it interesting that this overspending model relies upon consumer debt to support, which is exactly the model that imprisoned the Egyptians, and ultimately, the Hebrews under Pharaoh. (See Genesis 47:19.)

Some have accused Joseph of enslaving the Egyptians. I see it differently, where Joseph was the rescuer of their lives. The bondage came after a squandered seven-year bounty. The Egyptians knew of the coming famine; the whole country spent seven years preparing on a national scale. And finally, God Himself said *it was good* in Genesis 50:20. The seven abundant years of Joseph's stewardship were bounty years bearing increased crops. The increase was enjoyed by Egyptian and Hebrew alike. But only one nation lived in a Kingdom economy: Israel. The Egyptians ended up in bondage because they consumed all seven bountiful years. When times went lean, Joseph's plan saved their lives. Had they chosen to live like the Hebrews, with self-control and godly priorities, they would have also enjoyed provision during the final seven years of famine that followed. It is a clear demonstration of the two economies, one of Heaven and the other of Babylon. Revelation 18 makes interesting reading when learning that the very core of a Babylonian economy is slavery and human lives. (See Revelation 18:13.) Financial healing will train us to live as Joseph and not as a slave.

So, by way of overview, we plan our lives from a paradigm of generosity (say 10 percent minimum). Then we match savings (another 10 percent). This determines our living standard (remaining 80 percent in this example). Living on 80 percent will require that a person control her spending, which will require a proactive approach to lifestyle choice. I call this approach "Intention" or "Up-Living."

One more comment on the idea of generosity. We are all stewards—of money, of calling, of our bodies, of our thought-lives. God will ask us how we stewarded our relationship with Christ on that final day of accountability. Hearing "well done" will be based on how we stewarded our salvation. Stewardship is the basic rule of the Christian life. It is from the perspective of accountability that we should give. Giving cannot be a thoughtless casting of money at whatever charity happens to be passing before you at that moment. Learn how to give, when and where you should give, and to whom.

My sowing is not done in a capricious way, nor do I give from manipulation. I've learned how to say no, even in the context of giving. I understand that every dollar that comes into my hands is either seed or bread. Seed is for sowing and bread is for eating, and I am careful not to confuse the two. I avoid eating my seed (by living on what should be sown) and equally avoid sowing my bread (giving away what belongs to my family or others). I carefully spend and give and save, always around the priority of stewarding. Consider the idea of bread and seed carefully as you design your own life. And whatever you decide, be sure you are listening and deciding in faith as a cheerful giver.

DEFENSIVE AND OFFENSIVE

My last concept for financial healing relates to strategy. People regularly ask how to begin building wealth in a healthy way. I suggest you build in two stages—one defensive, one offensive. First, let's discuss the Defensive Stage.

Most Americans who struggle under a financial disease have no idea where their money goes or what their financial condition is, apart from a vague measure somewhere between good and not-so-good. They can't or won't live on a budget, choosing to wander aimlessly from paycheck to paycheck. If the paychecks stop, they just wander. I teach a popular home-budgeting skills class called "Prosperous Home." Every person who has taken that class hears me say, "If you aim at nothing, you're sure to hit it." That means wandering is not an option if you want healing in your finances. You need a plan, even if the plan changes continually. See your finances as a vehicle to reach your destiny as a supernatural steward; your budget is the plan to get from here to there. So, step one of the Defensive Stage is named Discovery.

Discovery requires the brave exercise of looking at your finances, especially when they're bloody. It requires new skills of creating and keeping a personal financial report called the Statement of Net Worth. The statement measures all of one's assets against all debts. The mathematical result of assets minus debts equals Net Worth, a key measure of wealth. There are many resources available to teach you about these ideas so I will not attempt it here. Let's just agree that the first step in building wealth is to know where you are currently and to build a target for where you and the Holy Spirit want to go financially.

The second step in the Defensive Stage is named Living Within Your Means. This applies the 80/10/10 model discussed earlier. Many of us begin our financial healing with a model closer to 90/10/0. Living Within Your Means focuses the effort applied to reducing the 90 percent down to your target goal of 80 percent. It is at this stage when people ask me now to change their percentages. There are as many methods and excuses as there are people when deciding how to control spending, but it all comes down to self-control. Self-control is a key element of financial health. Solomon wrote that a man who cannot control his spirit is like a city without walls (see Prov. 25:28). I summon my less-spiritual equivalent to Solomon's wise counsel when I see someone digging himself a hole financially. I tell him to apply the First Rule of Holes: Stop digging! You can't dig yourself out of a hole, so change something that isn't working. It hails back to the idea of living as a hero. Financial health implies that you *happen* to your finances; don't just let finances happen to you. Take control and make your money serve you. Money makes a terrible master but a perfect slave, so live intentionally. Remember, if you aim at nothing, you're sure to hit it...so

- ready,

- aim,

- fire!

The third step in the Defensive Stage is named Becoming the Bank. What this means is that in the course of life, you will likely face unexpected events. Some of those events are fun and pleasant; some are not. When the not-so-fun ones happen, they usually cost us money. So to live without a bumper to absorb those unexpected events is to live like a man who crosses streets with his eyes closed. He can hope and expect to cross safely, but sooner or later, there may be a bump in the road. And it may be him!

Everyone lives with a banking solution, even if we are not Becoming the Bank. This means somehow, some way, we always find a way through those unexpected financial emergencies. When you have an emergency fund, you can pay for the unexpected emergency from your own funds—you act as your own bank and pay the expense. When you don't have an emergency fund, you quickly pull that plastic out of your wallet, affectionately known as a credit card, and pay the bill. Visa or MasterCard are happy to become your bank because you now work for them. You will spend the following months working hard to pay the balance, plus a nifty interest rate. Welcome to Babylon; your life just became smaller until you pay off the credit card after the fact.

Breaking the cycle of debt requires these steps in order: Discovery, Living Within Your Means, and Becoming the Bank. And you must have these in place before moving on to the fourth step of Debt Freedom.

The fourth and final step in the Defensive Stage is paying off those old credit card balances. Doing so will free up considerable money and even improve your 80/10/10 model. Paying down debt may seem tedious, but God rewards a steward for faithfulness, not by the size of his savings (see Matt. 25:14-30).

Don't despise your slow and faithful payment plan, provided you are reducing debt every month at the highest rate possible. Many tools are available online and in books written by terrific authors. I recommend Dave Ramsey and Crown Ministries, both excellent resources with tools I teach and personally use.

These are the four steps in the Defensive Stage toward building wealth. The Offensive Stage continues these steps and adds interesting and challenging concepts like *multiple streams of income, home field advantages,* and *jeopardy money*. I cover these advanced ideas in other materials, so to keep to the scope of this chapter, I recommend visiting my website at www.prosperoussoul.com.

In Conclusion

God is not interested in money, but He *is* interested in our capacity to handle it. Whether we have lots of money or little makes no difference; we are called to live as examples of Jesus in either condition—one is not more sanctified than the other. After all, the beauty of a selfless life under God's hand rewards the rich and the poor alike. The only difference between the two is a matter of reach—a wealthy believer can give much more than a poor one. Both equally share the call to righteousness.

I mentioned early in the chapter that freedom is a spiritual power. I've learned that the power of freedom means little without the capacity for liberty. Freedom implies an escape; liberty implies multiple choices. Liberty requires the capacity to choose well between alternatives. Financial healing is like freedom—it contains the idea of escaping something, perhaps debt or destructive cycles. But healing means nothing apart from health, like financial healing means nothing without financial health. Develop financial health, which grants you the capacity to *carry* your money, to make it serve you and your God.

What do you do when you have choices? Are you afraid of free time? Are you afraid of wealth? If so, it is likely you are afraid of your own heart. Deal with that. Seek out a Financial Sozo. Find a coach or read my book, *Money and the Prosperous Soul*.

God is looking for a people He can trust with power. Money is power, and although He does not desire that all become rich, He does hope for a people who can live pure and righteously, regardless of the power He may assign. He wants a powerful people because the world deserves it; we owe them that.

In early history, Joseph was a Hebrew son who rose to become a father to Egyptian kings. Genesis 50:20 concludes that the evil and painful circumstances of Joseph's life were woven into a purpose—to save lives. Joseph became a source of life to a world of believers and unbelievers alike. And he did it through his stewardship of financial health.

It happened again with Solomon. As a result of Solomon's early fame, a queen from Sheba came to "see" if what she heard was true—and she was left "breathless." Solomon was a foreshadowing of what I call an *evangelism of jealousy*—possessing something the world would observe and desire.

Jesus did the same. He wasn't of the world, but the world found His way irresistible, so much so that Christianity was first called "The Way." There was a *way* about Him. And those who hated the way were those who wanted to restrain power. Sadly, and tellingly, it was the religious and political leaders who resisted Him the most. So, here we draw a line between a religious expression of Christianity and a relationship that attracts the world. The gospel of Jesus Christ will draw the thirsty. It will feed the hungry. Hidden here is part of a mystery: The gospel is attractive. It is beautiful. It is pure and artistic and creative. The gospel is inventive and essential, representing life. The gospel is not a club membership, but a treasure, one the world is hungry for, one Jesus would refer to as true riches.

> *Therefore, if you have not been faithful in the use of unrighteous wealth, who will entrust the true riches to you?* (Luke 16:11 NASB)

DECLARATION

Below is a declaration I wrote one night. It wasn't manufactured for this chapter. Instead it was an honest acknowledgement before my Maker of my gratitude. I am a prosperous soul; I pray you are inspired to heal your finances and thrive in your own journey as well. He can do it for you. Let's run together!

My days begin
with momentum.
Finally, alive!
After so many years.

I'm living my dream,
Working my favorite job,
Driving a car I prefer,
Eating the foods I want.

Married to the girl I love,
Living in the house I picked,
In the city I choose.
On the street I protect.

My friends are dear,
My children have grown—
Into the men I prayed for
Awaiting the wives of their youth.

My money serves me.
My future excites me.
My writing fulfills me.
My ministry thrills me.

My time with God
is tender. Real.
In silence He touches
Where I cannot reach.

***And** I work*
Hard!
I'm awake too late,
And I rise too early.

I sometimes worry—
But not for long.
I make mistakes—
But not too badly.

I am a prosperous soul.
Here in my Sabbath day.
Jesus is this for me.
And He doesn't miss a thing.

Beloved, I pray that in all respects you may prosper and be in good health, just as your soul prospers (3 John 1:2 NASB).

For more information:

For more of Stephen's books, manuals and materials, go to www.prosperoussoul.com.

INTELLECTUAL HEALTH
—CHAPTER 9—

And you shall love the Lord your God with all your heart, with all your soul, with all your mind, and with all your strength. This is the first commandment (Mark 12:30).

Hugh Ross is an astrophysicist who founded Reasons to Believe, an organization dedicated to discovering powerful new reasons that equip people to engage in the integration of science and Christian faith. I listened to him speak about the universe and the greatness of God. At one point, he used a mathematical figure that was so theoretical and astounding, my mind could not compute it. I looked behind me at Simon Munday, a Cambridge graduate in mathematics. Simon was beaming. He clearly "got it." I took Hugh's word for it and enjoyed the rest of the talk, the parts without numbers. What I came away with was this: had the universe been any older, younger, bigger or smaller, life on earth would not be possible. God had taken such care to make our universe habitable, at least on this one spinning globe. Hugh's talk thrilled and satisfied me. At home that evening I thought, *Wow. I just got to worship God with my mind! What joy!*

Loving the Lord is to be wiser than our teachers (see Ps. 119:99) and to be *"in all matters of wisdom and understanding...ten times better than all the magicians and astrologers"* (Dan. 1:20)—i.e., the wisest men of the day. We don't need to ignore our minds; we just need to have them renewed. Great believers of all ages—Einstein included—have made brilliant contributions to society. Our minds are a gift of the Lord. So I asked one who cultivates her brain well and knows how to ponder and worship God with her mind to write this chapter so we can celebrate the gift of our minds among His many benefits. —P.S.

With All Your Mind

by Chelsea Moore

in•tel•lect | ˈintlˌekt |

noun

the power of knowing as distinguished from the power to feel and to will : the capacity for knowledge

On the 26th of May 2007, I stood in cap and gown, self-consciously wondering if I was, in fact, a fraud. *I don't deserve a degree,* I thought. *Only experts and smart people deserve degrees.* I fidgeted with my tassels and thought about what would become of me, the college failure. While my siblings were off getting degrees in law and medicine, I sat with my head in the clouds, pretending to be some sort of poet, or essayist, and dreaming of being the next C.S. Lewis or Madeleine L'Engle. In that moment, I felt like every professor's worst nightmare—the student who hadn't really learned anything. I was the least intellectual person on the planet.

And then I was forced to walk forward with a swarm of other supposed intellectuals, dressed in long robes and funny hats, about to be paraded in front of our families and friends. If only they knew the truth! The doors opened, and I stopped breathing for a moment—until suddenly, my fear and doubt were stripped away. There stood our professors, the ones who had championed us for so long—each offering handshakes, smiles, high-fives, and congratulatory nods as we walked past. After four years of late nights, too much coffee, way too much procrastination, and an ongoing battle with self-doubt, I was rewarded with this: a company of people celebrating the gift of knowledge, education, and most importantly, the gift of intellect. The best part: they were celebrating that gift in me.

This is not about being smart. This isn't about the importance of higher education or what it means to be a good student. This certainly isn't about becoming an expert at, well, anything. This is about your intellect: a beautiful, valuable part of who you are. This is about you living to your fullest potential as a created being. Mostly, this is about you.

Now, you may be thinking *Why do I need to worry about intellectual health? I'm not an intellectual!* And so I thought, once. An intellectual can be defined as someone who is extremely rational, "a person who relies on intellect rather than on emotions or feelings."[1] While you may not consider yourself an intellectual, you do happen to have a very lively intellect, an intellect that needs some attention just like your body needs exercise.

Matthew 22:37 says, *"You shall love the Lord your God with all your heart, with all your soul, and with all your mind."* I don't think anyone would argue the fact that we all have a mind. We were, after all, created in the image of the greatest mind in all eternity. Your intellect is your mind. To be more precise, it is the part of your mind that gains and craves knowledge. You are, therefore, an intellectual being.

I learned to read just prior to entering public school, thanks to my parents' dedication to my education. And also thanks to the fact that I was desperate to keep up with my older brothers. I love to read. I've loved it since day one. And for as long as I can remember, I have had a bedroom full of books. When I was old enough to understand how to use the card catalogue at the library, I created my own card catalogue for my personal library. No one was allowed a book off my shelf without first checking it out. When I moved to Redding in 2007, I became the proud carrier of a Shasta County library card almost before I had the keys to my apartment. I simply love to read. It's how I gain knowledge, how I exercise my intellect. And in many ways, it is how I encounter God.

In looking at Matthew 22, the church certainly has pursued love with the heart and soul. However, what exactly does it look like to love the Lord with our minds? I've often heard people say that in order to allow God to give you an encounter, you must turn off your mind. Yes. And no. How can we love Him with our mind if we turn it off? Yet how can we encounter Him when our thoughts and hesitancies get in the way?

Turning off your mind in order to encounter God denies you the very unique experience of encountering Him with your intellect. It *is* important to push past the thoughts that can hold us back from experiencing a God who we don't fully understand, as long as we know that our mind is also an important part of our experience of Him. Our intellect craves the knowledge of Him just as our spirit craves His presence.

God delights in your intellect. He created it, organized it, and gave it all the potential in the universe. We often get confused and think that He only delights in us when we abandon our minds in order to let His Spirit flow through us. However, one doesn't necessarily relate to the other. He does delight in our abandonment, when we abandon ourselves *to* Him. He delights in our willingness to love Him using every aspect of our beings, everything that He gave us: body, spirit, soul, and mind.

Growing up, I never had any doubt in my mind that I would go to college. It was an unspoken understanding in my household: primary school, middle school, high school, university, and *then* the rest of your life. Now, please don't misunderstand me. My parents never put any pressure on me, or my siblings, to go to college. It was simply our understanding, our way of thinking, that college was a natural part of our intellectual journey. And I am, and always will be, grateful for that mindset.

Our Intellectual Journeys

Your intellectual journey may look very different from my own. But the fact is, you are on an intellectual journey. You have even experienced intellectual milestones: learning to tie your shoes, learning to read, graduating high school, starting your first business. I could go on and on. While formal education might not be structured to suit all minds, all minds were structured to learn. You can't stop learning. I tried once. Then I picked up the remote control and thought, *I wonder what's on TV*. I turned the TV on in order to learn the answer, and immediately had to give up on not learning. I began to see how valuable our minds really are. God designed us to learn: to think, to create, to build, to ask questions.

As a student, I was never very good at asking questions. I liked to observe, sit in the background and watch others interact. I liked to listen to other people's questions and then ask myself, *Is that what they really wanted to know?* After having spent most of my life in a classroom, I walked away from my school and promptly found my voice. And suddenly, I was full of questions. Good ones, I might add. I walked away from formal education with a newfound passion for learning. And I knew that I couldn't stop it. Nor did I want to.

Recognizing your journey as an intellectual being and then learning to value that aspect of who you are is the first step to intellectual health. Years ago, I was handed a devotional that was written for the YMCA, a guide to health for the body, mind, heart, and spirit. Day 10 of the booklet is a lesson on the value of being a lifelong learner. The author writes, "The wisest people realize that they can learn *something* from *anyone....* No one has lived the life you have lived. That makes you more of an expert on your experiences and insights than anyone else. You understand things that I don't. I understand things that you don't. And, someone with no education living in a grass hut on the opposite side of the world could teach us immensely about some aspect of life— if we cared enough to listen, and to learn."[2]

That spoke to me because I believe we should embrace lifelong learning.

The Church's Fear of Learning

Yet as believers, I think sometimes we fear learning. We fear that by opening our minds to learning, we will open our minds to something less than holy. Take a look at Romans

8:6: "*For to be carnally minded is death, but to be spiritually minded is life and peace.*" Somewhere along the line I believe we took this to mean that putting knowledge into our minds from a source other than the church or the Bible is to be carnally minded. And we began to refuse to gain knowledge from outside our Christian worldview.

My church experience taught me to value the missionary and the pastor, but to question the scientist, doctor, artist, and even teacher. Early in my time at college, I had a moment of doubt when I thought surely it was useless to spend so much time, energy, and money on an education that would get me no nearer to my goal of serving the Lord in some religious capacity. *I should just go straight to the mission field*, I thought, *or perhaps a Bible college.* Fortunately, the Lord did not let me off the hook that easily. Instead, I was challenged to rediscover my passion for writing and for language. And I began to learn that my thirst for knowledge and understanding was such a picture of His Kingdom that you could not separate the two. I experienced the joy of valuing the mind He gave me.

A few years ago, my mom gave me a book that confirmed the choice I had made to pursue knowledge in the form of education. It was a book about writing, published in 1985 by one of my favorite Christian authors, Bodie Thoene. There was one particular thought that, as I read it, made me feel as if I was suddenly given permission to succeed as a writer, and as an intellectual. Bodie wrote, "Christians cannot afford to be satisfied with anything second-rate. For too long we have made allowances for less than superior quality, comforting ourselves with the thought that if something was 'done in a good cause,' then a less stringent measure of performance could be applied. For this reason a world of unbelievers, whom we say we want to attract to Jesus, have come to associate Christianity with mediocrity."[3] I believe the mediocrity stems from the fear of learning, which stems from a lack of value for the intellect. In fact, to be carnally minded can be to ignore the fact that God created our minds, created us to explore His universe. Carnality is to ignore His handiwork in the world around us.

A Healthy Mind

I met my great aunt for the first time when I was 21 years old. Most of my extended family lives across the United States from where I grew up in the Pacific Northwest. Visits back to the Midwest happen rarely and were even more rare in my early life. So at 21, sitting in a musty living room at an assisted living facility, I tried my best to pretend that I wanted to be there. My mom and aunt fell easily into conversation with this woman who was a complete stranger to me, and so to pass the time, I picked up a book that was sitting on the coffee table. It was a book of memories that my great aunt had been writing, attempting to preserve her thoughts for the next generation. As I flipped through the pages, the scrawled handwriting became more and more illegible and the notes fewer and fewer. Finally, on one page near the back of the book was written a single line: "An active mind is a healthy one." Those words branded themselves in my memory.

It is one thing to have a healthy perspective of the intellect and people as intellectuals. But what is it to have a healthy intellect? We know that in order to be physically healthy, we must exercise and eat a balanced diet. In order to be spiritually healthy, we must pursue a relationship with God. So, how do we keep our minds healthy? Yet, even more than our minds, how do we maintain a healthy capacity for knowledge?

An active mind is a healthy one. Perhaps that is the ultimate key to maintaining a healthy intellect and a healthy value for the mind in general. But what does an active mind look like? For me, as you already know, reading is my answer to having an active mind. It is through reading that I introduce my mind to different worldviews and challenge my value system so that I am reminded of where I really stand in the depths of who I am—both heart and mind. This isn't the case for everyone.

It's about finding your balance. What stimulates your mind in a fresh way, in a way you don't experience on a daily basis? In my four years at university, I spent every spare moment listening to podcasts from Bethel and various other places, reading as much as I could, attending conferences, and going on mission trips. It was a fresh form of mental activity that was opposite to the literature and journalism that I was daily exposed to. Now that I've delved for 5 years into this culture—one that I absolutely love and value—I have to go outside of the four walls to find my balance.

I love discovering God's handiwork in unexpected places. Given my affinity for reading, I revel in finding His character in the most unlikely books, written by the most unlikely people. He's everywhere. He is everywhere because He created everyone, and everyone who creates will, without trying, reflect His image. While not everyone has accepted who He is, He still created their minds. And something happens when one of His creations, in turn, creates using the intellect He gave them: He is revealed.

Once we have a value for the intellect, for the mind that we were given, we suddenly have the freedom to see God in so much more of the world. I believe He absolutely thrills in the moments we recognize Him in the midst of our normal, humdrum lives. God is so much bigger than a name, so much bigger than a title. His glory is being revealed all over the earth at every moment, not because someone says the name "God," but rather because creation is breathing Him in and breathing Him out even now.

EXPERIENCING AND CELEBRATING YOUR INTELLECT

I don't think I will ever forget the way I felt the moment I stepped into the auditorium for my college graduation. My senior project overseer grabbed my hand as I walked past him and gently squeezed it, while whispering, "Well done." He was the professor who challenged me the most, fought against my fear as a writer and forced me to find my voice and dig deep to discover what I really believe about the world, my capability, and myself. It is to this professor that I will one day send my very first published work with a note of gratitude for pushing me to value my mind.

Discovering and valuing yourself as an intellectual is only the beginning of the journey. American author, Clarence Day, once wrote, "Information's pretty thin stuff, unless mixed with experience." It is one thing to value the mind; it is another thing to allow yourself to experience life using your mind at its greatest potential.

In my greatest moment of self-doubt as an intellectual, it was in the celebration of the gift of knowledge and understanding that my doubt and fear melted away. As a body, if we embrace and celebrate our intellect and our ability to learn and grow in knowledge, how much more will we be able to experience that very first commandment? *"Love the Lord your God...with all your mind"* (Matt. 22:37).

mind |mīnd|

noun

the element or complex of elements in an individual that feels, perceives, thinks, wills, and especially reasons

NOTES

1. *Dictionary.com,* s.v. "Intellectual," accessed October 10, 2012, http://dictionary.reference.com.

2. Caleb Anderson and YMCA of Tacoma-Pierce County, *Your Journey Toward Health* (Tacoma).

3. Brock Thoene and Bodie Thoene, *Writer to Writer* (Minneapolis, MN: Bethany House, 1990).

THE HEALTH OF CHILDLIKENESS

—CHAPTER 10—

But for you who fear My name, the sun of righteousness
will rise with healing in its wings; and you will
go forth and skip about like calves from the stall
(Mal. 4:2 NASB).

Now that I am—for sure—in the second half of my life,
I am starting to take notice of God's promises to keep me
young. Like countless others, I declare Psalm 103:1-5, especially emphasizing verse 5: "he renews my youth like the
eagle's." I think about how the Israelites in the dessert didn't
even need to get new shoes. That's how well the Lord pre-
served them (see Deut. 29:5). And I savor testimonies like
the one I read about a man in his 70s who, in obedience to
the Lord, began taking communion daily, after which his
hair became black again, and his skin renewed to that of a
younger man. I certainly have a part to play in preserving
my youth, but I can also trust the Lord to be the "health of

my countenance" (Ps. 43:5 KJV). And I can choose to stay young *inside*.

Recently I attended my high school reunion, and one lady told me that when she thinks of me, she remembers how easily I used to be able to just sink down into a split. She asked if I still could. "I wouldn't even think of trying to do that now," I laughed. But I could have still done that now had I kept it up all these years. Brittle bones and inflexible muscles don't have to be my portion. Neither does a stubborn, unbending heart. I can keep my childlike wonder and trust. It's a choice. Staying a child (in the right ways) is surely a sign of the health we can have in the Lord. I've seen the utter delight of a precious child in the face of a woman nearing 70, visiting here from England, drinking in the goodness of the Lord at every opportunity. Her eager joy sparkled with childlikeness. With her beaming face and twinkling eyes in mind, I write this chapter. —P.S.

Ever a Child

by Pam Spinosi

"You're a strange combination of intellectual and child," my sister's husband said as he passed me in the living room, lying on my stomach, feet in the air, poring over a Francis Schaeffer book on philosophy.

I liked that description. If we think about it, it fits us all in some ways. As we have seen from the previous chapter, the life of Jesus in us quickens our minds, makes them better (see Ps. 119:99). And the health of our brains is as important as—if not more so—than that of our bodies.

But there is another side to all of us: the kid inside, the silly, fun, innocent, whimsical little guy or gal we didn't just *used* to be but, if we are honest, still *are*, just in a taller package. I like that gal. I know Jesus does, too. He made that clear when He said, *"Verily I say unto you, except you be converted, and become as little children, you shall not enter into the kingdom of heaven"* (Matt. 18:3 KJV).

What is it about little children that so appeals to Him? Grab your lollipop, and let's have a peek.

CAPACITY FOR DELIGHT AND WONDER

Funny that the word we use for "something made impure" is *adulterated*. Our innocence is adulterated when we become cynical or blasé. Years ago, when I lived briefly in the then-Soviet Union, I encountered a five-year-old who had never seen popcorn popped before. I stayed with Martin and his mom, and I loved popping the corn for him and hearing his squeals and seeing his eyes brighten. Popcorn night always turned into a celebration.

And who wouldn't make the biggest fool out of himself—even in public—for the reward of a baby's smile or the sheer ecstasy of unrestrained, belly-felt baby giggles?

We are enjoined constantly to give thanks, rejoice, and glory in the Lord and His goodness. If we are thrilled at the sight of baby delight, how much more is our heavenly Father touched by ours when we express our delight in Him? My friend said to me, "I know my children. I know what they love, and I just can't help but to buy them the very thing I know will bring them joy. I think I may have spoiled them in that way." I thought that sounded like a very godly thing to do: delight in giving delight to your children. Who does that better than the Father of lights from whom comes every good and perfect gift (see James 1:17)? He gave us a hint that He is like that when He promised, *"Delight yourself in the Lord, and He will give you the desires of your heart"* (Ps. 37:4 NASB). What does our delight in Him look like to the One who dances over us with joy and wild abandon (see Zeph. 3:17)?

I love the way God's unusual and inexplicable manifestations reduce us all to children. Our church has experienced moments during our services when what appears to be gold dust has just floated down from the ceiling. Our reaction is always childlike awe. We scream and run toward it and crane our necks and, well, *delight*. One of the first nights it happened, a three-year-old broke away from her parents and dashed down the aisle after the angel that possibly only she could see. She got to the front of the church, looked up at a German man at the altar, and in perfect German (a language she does not know), said: "I love you."

For years we have at times seen feathers float down. We never take them for granted. They grab our attention, and we try to catch them, just as little children may try to capture a bubble floating by. We don't know why God does those things. Maybe He just wants to stir up our inner child a little because He misses him.

EASE IN FORGIVING

Another appealing thing about children is their boundless capacity for love, which results in their ready ability to forgive. Precious little ones are entrusted to less-than-perfect adults, who, even sometimes with the best intentions (and sometimes certainly not), do things that wound their souls or maybe even their bodies. Yet little children continue to love. Little children continue to forgive. Is it their guilelessness that causes their angels to always see the face of the heavenly Father (see Matt. 18:10)?

HUMILITY AND DEPENDENCE

Little ones know that they cannot completely take care of themselves, that they need others. Usually, they are humble about what they can and cannot do. They learn very early how to ask for help. I know that we need to regain that humble dependence on the Lord that we had for our parents when we were very small. Dependence on God keeps us safe.

I love the image of a young child sleeping contentedly with his head on the shoulder of his father, oblivious to his surroundings, perfectly secure. And I love the verse, *"But I have stilled and quieted my soul; like a weaned child with its mother, like a weaned child is my soul within me"* (Ps. 131:2 NIV).

GENUINENESS

Years ago, a friend of mine hung on her bathroom wall a full-page advertisement from a magazine, picturing a little baby girl, sitting contentedly in her "birthday suit," unbothered by her protruding baby belly. The caption read: "When was the last time you felt good about your body?" That stuck with me. Small children feel free to be themselves, and they are happy with the body, hair color, personality, facial features (you name it) they have been given. Those things are not an occupation for them. If they want to giggle loudly, they do. If they want to run or dance or squeal, they do. Of course they need to be taught appropriate behavior for various social situations, and they have to learn how to behave in human society; still it would be great if in their refinement process, they could retain a large bit of who they really are. As Theresa pointed out, somewhere in life, we "learn" that we are not what others expect in certain areas, and we suppress who we really were meant to be. I treasure genuineness when I see it. I love people who are "themselves," and I think we all love that. Even if we do not agree with someone, we like him or her to be real. Part of the freedom that the Lord brings to us is the freedom to go back to who we really were before we started trying to conform to others' expectations. I think the whole world benefits most from those who, through the redemption of Jesus Christ in their lives, come back to the original design God had for them, find their acceptance in Him, and take their place on the earth—the unique place reserved for them.

Trust and Readiness to Believe

What can we do to please God most? Trust Him. Believe Him. He loves that. That's the part of childlikeness that is most obvious. When I was a small child, I longed for a cat (something I did not get until I was ten). My cousin told me that if I found a four-leaf clover and put it in a book with a picture of a kitty in it, I would get a cat. That sounded like a great plan to me. I set about finding a four-leaf clover. Diligently I searched until one day I found one. I plucked it and tucked it in my little book about kittens and went to bed expectant. After all, the Tooth Fairy always delivered, and Santa Claus had never let me down.

The next morning the cat I fully expected to see was not there.

That experience was a disappointment only because I had believed. I couldn't be fooled by something like that again. While I'm glad of that, I don't want my sophistication regarding clovers and picture books to spill into my belief system toward my mighty and all-powerful living God. But faith may be for me the toughest area to remain childlike— and it is the most important.

Years ago, when I needed to sublet my apartment for the summer and had found an acquaintance interested in doing that, I was let down and completely insulted. After I had made all necessary arrangements, including making sure with city officials that she could park on the street near my apartment, Laura (not her real name) backed out because she did not trust in my assurances that I had done all that I promised or that it would work out. I had never experienced having someone blatantly question my reliability in such a hurtful way, even backing out of a promise to me. Immediately when that happened, I thought about the Lord and how He must have felt when I did the same to Him, when I failed from the heart to believe in His faithfulness, power, or goodness. *Oohh*. I would never have said that to Him, but by my actions I knew I had, at times, proven that as surely as Laura had proven to me her mistrust.

Ability to Have Fun

My Syrian grandmother, whom we called Sittie (Arabic for "grandmother"), and my niece, Hannah, share something special with me: we are the youngest child in our families. One of the most delightful people I have ever known, my Sittie lived six hours away from us, but we spent our summers with her and enjoyed her lavish, Middle-Eastern hospitality and ardent love of family. One winter, when I was about 23 and living in California, I spent Christmas alone with her in her West Virginia house. During my visit, we were snowed in for a couple of days, which meant no one could get to us and we could go nowhere. So we played. We laughed, joked, and ate *tutlee* (Turkish delight) without restriction. I had so much fun having Sittie all to myself. Born in a small village in turn-of-the-century Syria and not allowed to go to school, Sittie did not really know her birth date. She always just assumed she was ten years younger than she was. She also looked it, and she never lost her playful side.

About three years after my special Christmas with Sittie, I was living on the East Coast again, and I went to visit my sister in California. Hannah was three by then, and one evening she and I stayed home together while the rest of my sister's family went out to dinner. Hannah and I chatted and giggled on the tape recorder and had a great time. What astonished me later as I thought about it was realizing that my experience with Hannah was much like my experience with Sittie. It made no difference that one was three and the other, 83. We had a bond, and we shared the light-heartedness and free spirit of the youngest child. We were never going to lose touch with our inner child.

Come Out, Come Out, Wherever You Are!

So what can we do? How do we access our inner child?

Hang out with the child or children in your life and learn from them. One English businessman whom I met years ago has a great capacity for making others laugh because of the joy of the Lord he carries. He told me that when he went to Toronto years ago to receive from God in the renewal, at first he did not seem to be receiving. So he asked himself, "What would my three-year-old son do?" Then he stood up, and with a sweeping drinking motion, uttered, "Glug, glug, glug." And God poured out His presence on him, "ruining" him forever from being only serious and "adult." I once gave him a ride, and he made me laugh so hard that I was crying and driving with closed eyes, spurting tears.

Stir your wonder and delight as you look at God's handiwork or ponder His character. I have a huge coffee table book with gorgeous photos of exotic fish. They enchant and inspire me and remind me that I have a whimsical and creative side, too, like God. I take time to stare at dots on flowers and stripes on stones and to look into the knowing eyes of horses and guess what they are thinking. I love writing and painting stories for my nieces and nephews, and sometimes I check out children's books from the library—for myself.

Some of us just need to make time to play a little more.

A Healthy Appetite

Heather Thompson, who has worked with children internationally for 30 plus years, had one thing to add when I asked her to read this chapter: the insatiable hunger of children. She said they never think they've had too much. When she and her team pray for the children they minister to, they say, "If you want more prayer, go to the side." And they all go to the side for more prayer. After the meeting, they tell the children again, "If you want to receive more from God, go to the side, and we'll pray more," and 90 percent of them normally go. The little sponges receive easily and always want more. She said they don't put limits on what they can receive; they are "greedy" in the right sense of the word. Recently, Bill Johnson has been speaking a lot about the gift of hunger, about how—whether it is physical or spiritual hunger—it is a sign of health, a sure sign of *sahtein*. So I conclude with this thought: be like a child; stay hungry.

Sahtein!

About the Authors

Chris Gore

Chris is currently the Director of Healing Ministries for Bethel Church. While having an unquenchable hunger for His presence, Chris' passion is to see the church walk in a Kingdom mindset and see ordinary saints equipped to walk in extraordinary exploits by releasing the Kingdom through healings and miracles. His heart is to see churches, cities, and nations transformed.

Pam Spinosi

Pam Spinosi serves Bethel Church in two roles: Testimony Writer and International Student Liaison for BSSM. A college ESL and English instructor by profession, she teaches writing classes at BSSM, edits books and documents, and presents at Bethel's Writing Unto the Glory Conference, which she launched and has organized four times since 2006.

Deborah Stevens

Deborah Stevens is on the Operations Management Team at Bethel Church in Redding Ca. She has been the Events and Guest Ministries Director for the past 10 years. She was born, raised and lived in Canada before moving to Redding, CA in the fall of 2002. Deborah is passionate about seeing people go deeper in their relationship with God and with one another through knowing God and through continual encounters with the tangible, relentless, fiery love and glory of God. Deborah is one of the authors in two of the Bethel's books titled *An Apple for the Road Wisdom For The Journey & Health in Every Realm*. You may contact Deborah at deborahs@ibethel.org.

Theresa Dedmon

Theresa Dedmon has a traveling ministry both in the United States and abroad which focuses on equipping and activating churches to step into their supernatural destiny. She activates churches in how to touch their community through creative expressions and love. She empowers people to go after their dreams, and teaches how God's supernatural creative power can be released in every part of church life as well as worship. She has a BA in Psychology and minor in Biblical studies and has been in pastoral ministry for over 25 years. She is currently on staff at Bethel Church in Redding, California, where she leads the Creative Arts ministries there and in their School of Supernatural ministry. She is a sought after conference speaker who releases people to be set free to walk in supernatural creative power. She has written a manual, called "Cultivating Kingdom Creativity." She ministers with her husband, Kevin Dedmon and with her 3 children, Chad, Julia, and Alexa.

You can read more about her at :

Theresadedmonministries.com

Kevin Dedmon

Kevin Dedmon has a traveling ministry focused on equipping, empowering, and activating the Church for supernatural evangelism through signs and wonders, healing, and the prophetic. He earned a Master's degree in church leadership from Vanguard University, and has been in full-time ministry for more than 25 years. He and his wife are part of Bethel Church staff in Redding, California.

Dawna De Silva

Dawna De Silva is the founder and co-leader of the Sozo Ministry birthed at Bethel Church. Whether training, teaching, shifting atmospheres, or ministering prophetically, she releases people, churches, and cities into new vision and freedom. No matter how traumatic the wounding, Dawna ministers with authority and gentleness, imparting hope and healing.

Stephen De Silva

Stephen De Silva serves as CFO and member of the senior leadership team for Bethel Church in Redding, California. He teaches on mastering finances from the biblical truth of identity. His titles include *Money and the Prosperous Soul, Financial Sozo*, and *Stewardship Foundations*. His latest project is entitled *Prosperous Home*.

Leslie Taylor

Leslie Taylor is the Director of the Pastors on Call ministry at Bethel Redding and a home business entrepreneur. Prior to moving to Redding to attend BSSM, she was a police officer in Colorado for eight years, and prior to that, a marriage and family therapist. Leslie is married to Tom and has two grown sons, a daughter-in-law, and four grandchildren. Her website is: http://www.LiveRadiantly.com.

Matthew DiMarco

Matthew DiMarco and his wife Trish are called, gifted, and anointed to mother and father this generation of revivalists. Over the past five years, their home has been open to BSSM students from various places in the United States and around the world. Together Matt and Trish equip young people to experience and achieve successful family.

An Invitation

There! You have traveled through this whole book with us. But come to think of it, we wrote from the point of view of those who have received the greatest gift of health there can be: a clear conscience through faith in the Lord Jesus Christ.

We didn't want you to put the book down without letting you know that you, too, can have that—along with the unsurpassed joy of knowing God—which, in all truth, is the beginning of healing in any area of our hearts or lives.

The apostle Paul, in the book of Hebrews, chapter 10, verses 19 and 22 wrote:

> *So, friends, we can now - without hesitation - walk right up to God ... So let's do it—full of belief, confident that we're presentable inside and out.* (MSG)

That is what Jesus did for you: Jesus brings us into relationship with God. How? He gave Himself as payment for our sins, making us presentable inside and out. In this way, we can come into God's presence as a friend. After trading his life for ours, erasing our sin, Jesus rose from the dead so that we could walk a new life, a kind of life that is a gift from God.

Now, through Christ you can experience that life, everything written in this book, and much more!

If that is something you want, go ahead and pray this prayer from your heart:

> *Lord Jesus, I believe that you are the Son of God, that you can wash away all sin. You died for me and you rose again. I ask you to forgive me for any sin in my life, whether known or unknown. I ask you to come into my heart and give me new life. I give myself to you and trust you to change my heart and lead me into a loving relationship with the Father, you the Son and the Holy Spirit.*

That prayer, prayed from the heart, always gets answered. It's your way to say yes to God. Yes to His beautiful goodness and love having a way into your life. Yes to getting to know Him and also finding out who He created you to be. His plan for you is greater than you can imagine!

Keep going. It's only the beginning. Read the Bible and initiate relationships with other believers. Start your journey with the living God today.